Now They Tell Me

50 Life Lessons I Didn't Learn in School

By Ed Harris

First Edition December 2013
ISBN 13:   978-0-9898076-4-7
ISBN 10:   0989807649

This book is based on actual events. However, certain names have been changed.

Biblical quotations are from the online Hebrew/English version of the Jewish Bible:
www.jewishvirtuallibrary.org/jsource/Bible/jpstoc.html

To my parents, Anita and Richard Harris. The lessons you taught me are priceless.

Other Books by Ed Harris

*Let's Pretend We're Christians and Play in the Snow:
The Adventures of a Jewish Dad*

Fifty Shades of Schwarz

Put It On The House

Murphy's Bed

"What a piece of work is a man!"

Hamlet, Prince of Denmark by William Shakespeare

Contents

Preface

This book is about how formal education failed me, despite the fact I generally did well in school for most of my academic career. Fortunately, they did not take any points off for being obnoxious; otherwise the statement above might not be true. As a student, I earned good grades, got high scores on standardized tests like the SAT, and accumulated a number of honors and awards. (I am sorry if that sounds like bragging; I'm just trying to set the context for what follows.)

My dedication to studying resulted in an undergraduate degree and an MBA, both from well-regarded universities. Once college catapulted me over the campus walls and into the rest of my life, I considered myself smart and well-educated.

But my self-confidence shattered like a delicate Lalique vase being battered with a sledgehammer as I tried to make my way in the so-called "real world." I discovered that despite the grade point average I had been so proud of, I was often a blithering idiot outside of a classroom.

My nearly infinite capacity for being an imbecile is not helped by the fact that I am a man. The male brain can often be remarkably dense, adding to the challenge of being "street smart" as opposed to "book smart."

Throughout the course of my life, I have made dumb mistake after dumb mistake, each time slapping my forehead and wondering how I could have been clueless. Finally, I realized I wasn't entirely at fault: public education woefully prepares us for adult life.

Schools are self-contained little universes, with limited capacity for correcting their mistakes or making improvements. In the business world, when a venture doesn't succeed as planned, such as a big-budget movie that bombs in theaters, the lack of ticket buyers is pretty obvious. If a restaurant sits empty, it eventually closes; same with a store that doesn't sell its wares. Flops are allowed to flop, and then it's back to the drawing board. In the school world, harebrained concepts and bad practices can live on forever because there are no genuine customers except taxpayers held captive to the system. To consider how long things that make no sense can persist in the artificial realm of education, note that we still close schools in the summer so kids can help out on the family farm, even though the US Department of Agriculture reports that only about 2 percent of the nation's population live on farms, a number that has been in consistent decline for the past 100 years.

But, since John Q. Public maintains the cash flow, there is no incentive for schools to adapt or improve. The outside world constantly evolves but schools remain static. With the passage of time, formal education, like a penguin's wings, is increasingly less relevant to the requirements of daily life. Poor saps like me, and I suspect many of the rest of us, are stuck with the consequences.

In the hope that I can help others avoid future disappointment, I have decided to chronicle the most important aspects of the real world where school leaves us unready for the future. Perhaps if I share my own history of lumps and bruises, I can help others sidestep similar unfortunate consequences. I hope you gain valuable information and enjoy the ride along the way.

Like me, this work is a combination of data and opinions. In regard to the various facts, statistics, and figures, I am solely responsible for any errors, omissions, or misstatements. In regard to opinions, they are entirely my own. It is not my intention to give offense—on the other hand, it's hard to make an omelet without breaking eggs.

The creation of a book is a team effort. In my case, I rely heavily on the support, insights, good judgment and patience of my wife, Anne. As always, I am grateful for her help. And the kids keep me on my toes at all times.

Ed Harris

Website: www.edharrisauthor.com
Facebook: www.facebook.com/EdHarris.Author
Twitter: www.twitter.com/EdHarrisAuthor

Chapter 1: Things Are Better Today

One of the things you constantly hear from adults, especially authority figures such as teachers, is that the current generation of kids is rotten compared to when those same teachers, by extraordinary coincidence, were kids themselves. If the adults are to be believed, the past was truly golden: less crime, more respectful youth, and an orderly and civilized society. Even the music was supposedly better, which is a claim that has been made by every generation since the first caveman bounced a stick off of a rock and liked what he heard.

Lies, all lies.

In the "good old days," America was infected with many grave sins, racial discrimination among the worst. During my childhood in the 1960s I closely followed baseball, including many great African-American players who were then current stars, like Hall-of-Famers Willie Mays and Hank Aaron. They would sometimes be complimented, in a patronizing way, "a credit to their race." Apparently, they should have been further lauded, in addition to their athletic exploits, for resisting the temptation to hold up liquor stores on their way home from the ballpark.

Even though the Civil Rights Movement demolished legal barriers, it took a long time for social attitudes to catch up. To many whites, a polite, articulate, law-abiding black person was something to be celebrated, supposedly an exception to the general rule. Real progress came slowly.

No, life is better today, unless you'd like to bring back a set of practices that most people would consider repugnant, such as openly tolerated discrimination against blacks. Let me modify my claim about how life has improved. It's better now for everyone, except the racists. Even homophobes are having a rough time of it these days.

Chapter 2: Don't Be Afraid to Be Wrong

One of the problems with school is the emphasis on there being only one single exact right answer to every question. This creates a way of thinking that is dysfunctional in adult life because often there are many different paths to the truth. The answer key to exams may reflect a certainty that is black and white, but most of life contains shades of gray. And even when things seem obvious, the correct answer might change over time. For example, rock and roll music was once considered a sign of moral decay and sexual degeneracy. Now it's gone corporate. Recent Super Bowl halftime acts have featured Beyoncé, The Black-Eyed Peas, Madonna, and The Who. By contrast, at the first Super Bowl, held on January 15, 1967, at the Los Angeles Memorial Coliseum, the performers included The University of Arizona Symphonic Marching Band and The Anaheim High School Drill Team.

A common, recurring development of the last 4,000 years of human civilization is for older adults to complain about new ways of doing things. I recall in business school, we reviewed a case study about a large bank that implemented a major restructuring to improve the efficiency of their operations. I studied for my MBA from 1983–85, so the material was probably written a few years earlier, in the late 1970s or early 1980s. The bank decided they needed an overhaul of their business processes, so they decided to hire a senior finance executive from a global manufacturing company, even though he wasn't a career banker. One of the interesting aspects of the case study was that after the potential new CEO was offered the job, he told the board of directors he wanted to discuss it with his wife and see if she supported a family relocation to New York. This was, at the time, regarded as a major departure from how business was normally conducted.

For example, there was an inside joke at IBM that the letters stood for "I've Been Moved." If you worked at "Big Blue" and were offered a promotion, there was no discussion with the family. You simply went home and told your wife to pack. The idea that the missus should be involved in the decision was as unthinkable as a simple parishioner asking the Pope if they shared similar opinions on the concept of purgatory.

Fast forward to today. I imagine that a husband who came home from work one day and said, "Honey, I accepted a promotion and we'll be on our way to Dallas next week" might find himself banished to the couch come bedtime. The realities of modern life and the social attitudes that go along with it constantly change.

So the next time you are sure you have all the right answers, just wait, because before you know it, they'll be wrong.

Chapter 3: Experts Aren't

In the 1960s, one of the bestselling books was *The Population Bomb*, in which author and Stanford Professor Paul Ehrlich predicted rolling global waves of mass starvation as a result of overpopulation. The future was going to be a giant disaster for humanity. In fact, most of his major predictions failed to materialize. Fertility rates in developing nations, the countries supposedly the most responsible for the "bomb" that was going to destroy humanity, plummeted. According to the World Bank, the fertility rate in India, which a generation ago was perhaps the poster child for global poverty, has fallen by nearly half since 1980, from 4.7 births per 1,000 women to 2.6 today.[2] Fertility rates in Brazil (1.81) and Thailand (1.56) are now lower than France (2.0) and Sweden (1.98).[3] One the biggest challenges for several industrial nations, such as Germany (1.36) and Japan (1.39), is the fear of a population bust, as birth rates have fallen to levels that point to future population decreases. Over the same time period, living standards rose around the globe.[4] Yes, there is still a lot of poverty, which is regrettable, but the average level of calories consumed by the world's population has gone up substantially, not down, since Ehrlich's doomsday scenario, with the rate of increase in developing nations exceeding that of industrialized economies.[5]

In the 1970s, environmentalists took the same message and made it even gloomier—the air and water around us were being poisoned, and we were running out of natural resources, in particular fossil fuels. A leading group of intellectuals known as the "Club of Rome" predicted a long-term decline in living standards as the world gradually ran out of everything (except, I suppose, dire predictions).

Once again, wrong, wrong, wrong. *The Wall Street Journal* reported that oil production in 2012 rose in the United States by more than any year since 1859, the earliest date from which records have been kept by the petroleum industry, and an even greater increase is predicted for 2013.[6] The Saudis are starting to get nervous. Economic growth in developing nations has been remarkable, especially in places such as China, Brazil, India, and Korea. The air and water in western nations are cleaner, not dirtier. The EPA reported air pollution in the United States declined by 59 percent over the 20-year period from 1990 to 2010.[7] You can even swim in New York's East River, provided you avoid the victims of organized crime hits bobbing in the current.

The next time an "expert" predicts with great certainty that we are all doomed due to global warming, or because we will be overrun by immigrants, or the government will collapse in a last gasp of fiscal insolvency, you can count on one thing for sure: his or her crystal ball isn't any clearer than yours.

Chapter 4: Not Ready for a Restaurant

I came home from a year of backpacking at age 19, determined to save up enough money to finance another extended trip overseas. Unfortunately for my parents, this plan forced their plans to send me to college to be indefinitely postponed. I moved back into my childhood bedroom, juggled multiple part-time jobs, and held discretionary expenses close to zero. I managed to save nearly my entire combined take-home pay of $100 a week. I took service standards to new lows as a waiter at a restaurant located at the Molly Pitcher rest stop, near exit 8A of the New Jersey Turnpike. (As the New York joke goes, when someone tells you they are from New Jersey, the response should be, "Oh really, what exit?")

My transgressions were legion. I forgot orders completely amid busy rushes, which left frustrated patrons to give up and return to their cars in hope of better luck farther down the road. I dropped a scoop of ice cream on the floor near the freezer in the back of the kitchen and then picked it up and put it back on the plate once I determined no one had seen me. I also had my employee pin out of place on a day the CEO of the parent company was scheduled to visit, which led a coworker to fear that I might be fired on the spot if he saw me on his inspection.

I also had a particular issue with toothpicks. The restaurant served club sandwiches with decorative toothpicks inserted through the center of the bread and festooned with brightly colored foil at the top. As a result, a part of my brain learned the rule (as if I was a pigeon in a Skinner box trained to peck for food pellets) that at our establishment "some dishes come with a toothpick sticking out of them." The menu consisted of items that were either salty and greasy or overly sweet, and which all shared the distinction of being something one would only eat if stuck on a New Jersey toll road with a single food provider holding an exclusive contract. Given how awful the quality was, I paid no mind if the toothpick added any appeal to the dish it accompanied. With or without any decorative sliver of wood, the fare still looked like an unappetizing plate of empty calories one would avoid eating except under the duress of turnpike travel.

In addition to the club sandwiches, we also kept individually sliced pieces of pie in a refrigerated case with a toothpick stuck in the middle of each. I later realized that the toothpick's purpose was not to distract the patron from the unappetizing mass of congealed industrial dough and syrupy goo that had just been placed in front of them but to keep the plastic wrap from adhering to the crust. More than one customer unfortunate enough to be seated in my section remarked they had never seen a piece of pie served with a toothpick stuck into it, to which I replied, "Neither had I, until I started working here." My understanding is that the chain which ran this restaurant has long since pulled out of the turnpike food service business to focus on hotels. A wise decision.

Had I continued in this job much longer, I would inevitably have been fired for my bad service, despite having not been seen by the big boss on the day of his visit. Beating management to the punch, I quit instead, taking a busboy job at a popular steak and seafood restaurant in Princeton. Their strategy was to get patrons bloated on the relatively low-cost unlimited salad bar served on full-size dinner plates, thereby encouraging hearty portions, along with a loaf of freshly-baked bread and a tureen of soup. Most customers would consume an amount of salad equivalent in size to a Halloween pumpkin suitable for carving into a jack-o-lantern, along with half a loaf of bread and a couple of servings of soup, dulling their appetites before being served the smaller (and higher cost) entrée.

One of my responsibilities as busboy was to open up several massive institutional-size cans of the day's soup, empty them into a vat, and then put the vat into a warmer in the kitchen so that it would be ready to serve when the restaurant opened. On one unfortunate day, after I filled up the vat, I dropped it onto the floor in the kitchen and spilled about 500 servings of soup in the process. That incident doomed any hopes I may have had of ever rising in the ranks to waiter. Other busboys got promoted on the basis of seniority while I languished at the very bottom of the hierarchy. One day the assistant manager explained to me in passing, in regard to how he made personnel decisions, that in the restaurant industry it was really important to emphasize performance. I may have been a naïve youth, but I had enough horse sense to realize his comments translated to my chances of promotion to waiter being about even with that of hell freezing over.

And so it went. I endured a dirty job bussing tables in return for low pay and meager tips. After a few months, I had saved up enough money from the restaurant and my other two jobs to resume backpacking. The trip my menial labor financed led to, among other things, marrying the cute Dutch girl next door to me on a kibbutz, which proves that good can come out of bad. Busboy was my last position at a restaurant, and the industry must have heaved a collective sigh of relief when I took my talents, such as they were, into the world of business and finance.

Chapter 5: Bob Dylan Was Right

Pot is not nearly as bad as its critics claim. It's not just that the potential harm is grossly exaggerated—think of the movie *Reefer Madness*—but the benefits are probably greater than anyone ever realized. Not only does ganja have a whole bunch of legitimate medical uses, such as relieving pain, nausea, and other negative side effects for seriously ill people, but it also can boost appetite and just plain cheer you up. And even for ordinary, healthy folks who aren't in agony or trying to recover from depression, having fun is fun, and something you just can't get enough of. Besides, Cheech & Chong movies are unwatchable unless you have at least a mild buzz. Cannabis is now legal for personal consumption in two states— Colorado and Washington—and approved for medical use in about another 25 or so. People seem to have finally figured out that to put people in jail for the possession of Mary Jane is outrageously stupid and a poor use of taxpayer resources. It seems inevitable that the legal code will inevitably catch up with social attitudes. And with Twinkies back on the market, the timing of a pot boom couldn't be any better.

Chapter 6: Marry Young

We are all influenced by our surroundings. I was raised in a comfortably middle-class family, with a Jewish emphasis on education and learning. The values we embraced, of studying hard in preparation for the future, have become widespread across American society. As a result, more people attend college and wait until they establish their careers before they get hitched. This might not be the only factor: changes in traditional attitudes toward morality mean "getting any" was a lot harder for guys in the era of black-and-white television, and marriage carried with it certain sexual benefits that are probably less germane today. This change in behavior and widespread acceptance of doing the horizontal mambo outside of the bonds of holy matrimony is shown in the steady rise of the age of first marriage.

According to Pearson Education, publisher of the website Infoplease, data from the US Census Bureau shows that the average age of first marriage has gone from 22.8 years of age for men and 20.3 years for women in 1950 to 28.2 for men and 26.1 for women in 2010.[8] If this trend continues, our grandchildren will begin marrying in their mid-30s, about the same time their knees begin to get creaky and the human body begins its gradual transformation from youth to something grimmer.

But is it a good idea to wait? The choice to defer the establishment of your wedding registry until you work at a job that offers a 401(k) and Internet access to alleviate the boredom seems logical enough. By the time you are through your mid-20s and the dreaded big "three-oh" is on the horizon, much of your life's trajectory is set. You've probably completed your formal education and have begun to establish yourself in the work world. You have also likely gotten much of the prolonged partying that college students and young adults enjoy out of your system. And chances are you have had several sexual partners, which means you seek to enter relationships with a balance of both physical attraction and potential compatibility. With this moderation of the first heat of sexual ripening, you are likely to become more prudent in your judgment, but that need not always be the case. The term "trophy wife" wouldn't even exist but for the phenomenon of middle-aged men who trade up to new arm-candy once they achieve sufficient financial success.

But there is one big problem with the choice to bide one's time to exchange "I do's" until the age you first start to pay serious attention to those erectile dysfunction commercials: the older you become, the more set you get in your ways, and the pickier you get in your habits. As you continue to build your life as a single person, the harder it becomes to figure out how to make the adjustments required to intertwine your day-to-day existence with someone else. Everything, from simple issues like what you will have for dinner, and where and when you will eat it, to more complex matters such as the home you live in, become a negotiation. When you're single, if you want to scarf down a burrito in your car while driving home from work and then stop at the driving range to hit a bucket of golf balls, no one will stop you. Add a significant other to the equation, and it's no longer so simple.

"Oh, you wanted to go out tonight? I thought we

were getting together with Mandy and Bikram for drinks tomorrow." Eventually, marriage starts looking like the plans for a corporate merger. Together with your potential mate, you've got two residences, two sets of furniture, two different career paths, and two separate lives that need to be combined into one. How to make that combination work is as complex as any business deal, maybe even more so given the emotions involved. Which regional fulfillment center will be closed in the consolidation, Phoenix or Albuquerque? Who gets the corner office at headquarters? Which set of living room furniture do we take to Goodwill?

Consider the advantages of marrying young, like my wife and I did at ages 20 and 21 respectively. We were flat broke, with no college experience, and we considered adulthood a phase of life we had yet to enter. We felt like, and genuinely were, kids. At our wedding celebration in Amsterdam, in the summer of 1978, my new bride tried to pick the lock on the bathroom door with her seven-year-old niece and four-year-old nephew in the hope they could catch me with my trousers down around my ankles as I was busily engaged with urgent matters. I bet that this kind of thing doesn't happen when you tie the knot at age 41 instead of 21.

One of the great things about marrying at today's legal drinking age is that, if you indeed have met the right person, as I was fortunate enough to do, then you get to spend more of your life with them. And the time you spend together, in your early 20s, is exactly when you will have the greatest sense of fun and adventure. To a certain extent, you grow up together.

I recall one particular lunch with my parents at their country club. The table next to us was filled with middle-aged businessmen. We happened to overhear one of them say, "So who do you think shot J.R.?", a reference to a plot gimmick from the TV show *Dallas*, when a season ended with bad guy J.R. Ewing being shot by an assailant out of camera range. The idea was to keep viewers on tenterhooks for an entire summer before the shooter was revealed in the first episode of the following season. And despite the gimmick, it worked, and believe or not, there was once a summer where all of America asked, "Who shot J.R.?"

After the lunch, on the drive home, Anne and I were both surprised that adults talked about frivolous TV shows. We overestimated the level of maturity of the adult world, a sign of how ridiculously unprepared we were for marriage We didn't even know what constituted regular adult conversation.

We had no sophisticated tastes and preferences that we had to blend in together. We didn't have to argue about which restaurants to eat dinner at because we couldn't afford to go out. We couldn't afford almost anything. We spent our 20s going to college and graduate school, our 30s raising small children, our 40s raising older kids, and now in our 50s we finally can see the finish line, as our youngest son, Izzy, enters high school. (Although we'll likely be too financially, emotionally, and physically depleted to fully enjoy our free time once we have it.)

Meanwhile, our daughter also married at the insanely young age of 21. Did she make a mistake? I don't think so. Like my wife and me, she now has the opportunity to build a life together with the man that she loves. I don't want her to copy her parents too completely because that would mean a wait of another decade for grandkids. I think I'm old enough to be a grandpa right now.

Chapter 7: Money Doesn't Buy Happiness

A couple of years ago, on a rainy Sunday afternoon (we have a lot of those in Seattle), I took Izzy to the movies in order to alleviate what might have become a fatal case of boredom. From a distance, I noticed a local billionaire that I had met on several occasions in prior business dealings and saw that he was with his young son as well. Even if you are stupendously wealthy, damp and dreary Sunday afternoons in Seattle are still a drag.

Many years ago, by coincidence, I discovered that among the patients of my dentist was a prominent local Microsoft multibillionaire. Even if I was one of the wealthiest men on the planet, I could not possibly have received better dental care. Imagine that. Plus I was married to the woman of my dreams. All of which led me to conclude that indeed money does not buy happiness.

Chapter 8: Money Can Stave Off Unhappiness

In the previous chapter, I argued the belief that wealth leads to happiness is an illusion. However, that doesn't mean the opposite, being poor, is a ticket to contentment. Some extra cash in the bank can't make you happy, but it can help keep unhappiness at bay.

When I was in college, one day in a marketing class, we had a discussion about the telephone business. This was years before cell phones came along. The professor remarked that the industry had a 90 percent market penetration rate which meant 10 percent couldn't afford phone service.

One of the students in the class was incredulous. "There isn't anyone," he protested, "who can't afford a phone."

What he really meant was, "I come from a middle-class background and attend college. There is no one in my personal universe that I am aware of who can't afford telephone service. Therefore, I have concluded, from this small sample size, in regards to the entire population of the United States, that *everyone* can afford a phone."

This fellow schoolmate of mine failed to realize he was limited by the paucity of his own experience. In fact, there is a segment of the population that is desperately impoverished. There are homeless people who sleep under freeway underpasses. (I might join them if I don't sell enough copies of my books.) There are millions of people who live on the very edge of subsistence.

For example, according to a 2011 study entitled "The Dental Access Gap" funded by the W.K. Kellogg Foundation, only about 70 percent of the United States population has regular access to dental care because they don't have enough finances to pay for it.[9] When poor people who cannot afford to see a dentist have a toothache, their tooth hurts and they take aspirin. When it gets really bad, their teeth start to fall out of their mouth. I think a little bit of extra money might improve their lives.

Beyond a certain level, surplus cash clearly does not make you any happier. More possessions can also mean more headaches. Meals out in restaurants can be fun. However, on a daily basis it is no longer a special event but just another humdrum part of life. Above a certain level, money helps prevent a lot of misery. My advice in financial matters is to aim for somewhere slightly above the middle, where you have material comfort but don't have to worry about the impression you make on anyone else. Leave the headaches of the rich to the rich.

Chapter 9: God Is Male

Here is a simple thought experiment for you. If you ignored the obviously patriarchal language of the Bible and just had to guess, what gender would you think is appropriate for God? Well, you might start by considering that for most of our evolutionary history, we lived primitive hunter-gatherer lifestyles. You couldn't pick up the phone to order a pizza or call 911 in an emergency. And one thing that pre-modern humans certainly didn't have access to were modern toilets or running water. If you had to go to the bathroom, then you simply walked a few steps away from the encampment into the underbrush, hoisted up your animal pelt, and relieved yourself. And as anyone who has ever gone on a long hike or a camping trip has ever noticed, men are at a decided advantage to women for the more frequent type of bathroom visits. We simply stand upright and casually void our bladders, manhood in one hand and smart phone in the other. Women, meanwhile, have to squat in an extremely undignified position. And this was the human condition for 99-plus percent of

27

our existence and still is today for people living outside of civilization—those poor souls who do not have access to *Family Guy*.

Now I ask you, can you possibly imagine a deity who created the universe and gave men such a decided advantage over a critical part of survival without being male himself?

I rest my case.

Chapter 10: God and Religion Are Not the Same

It's been a bad 500 years for organized religion in Western society. Truths that were once taken to be immutable, such as the earth being at the center of the universe or created a mere 6,000 years ago, have been proven wrong by science. The universe is exceedingly larger and older than our limited human brains can grasp.

The Catholic Church and other Christian denominations for many centuries insisted on the Bible being understood as a literally accurate record of the natural history of the cosmos. Like an argument over which is the best *Star Wars* movie, the debate still can arouse strong passions today. However, the track record of religion vs. reason regarding discrepancies between Scripture and scientific discovery has generally been lopsided, like that of the perpetually overmatched Washington Generals against The Harlem Globetrotters. Yes, some people claim the reason dinosaur fossils appear in layers of sediment is because they were deposited there by the receding waters of the biblical flood. However, this fanciful notion is not taken seriously by legitimate scientists.

Another issue that the major faiths have grappled with is how to deal with their ancient prejudices. The dominant religions of today originally developed when slavery, the oppression of women, total warfare, and other great evils were tolerated as integral parts of existence. It was taken for granted as simply the way one did things a few thousand years ago, that when you conquered an enemy on the battlefield, you sacked the major cities, destroyed the temples, killed all the men, took all the young women as sexual possessions, and enslaved everyone else. Unless you decided to simply annihilate everyone in your path instead. That was just the normal state of affairs in the ancient world and even the Jewish Bible commanded the Israelites to wipe out the inhabitants of Canaan as they entered the Promised Land.

> *Howbeit of the cities of these peoples,*
> *that The Lord thy God giveth thee for an*
> *inheritance, thou shalt save alive nothing*

that breatheth, but thou shalt utterly

destroy them: the Hittite, and the

Amorite, the Canaanite, and the Perizzite,

the Hivite, and the Jebusite . . .

(Deuteronomy, 20:16-18)

Religion has also strived to avoid change. All prior practices, even those of questionable moral value like barriers against women, at one time or another have been termed "traditions." And great crimes like the oppression of gays demonstrate that old hatreds die hard.

What is often lost in this debate is that while religions claim to be based on belief in God that does not necessarily mean He reciprocates and believes in them. You might insist that the Lord has commanded you to burn witches at the stake, a common practice for much of European history. But the Creator might disagree that He ever sent that memo. Even self-proclaimed atheists often acknowledge a spiritual dimension to the universe. But to profess a belief in God does not mean that you speak for Him. If you think slavery was a pretty good idea or gays should not be allowed to participate fully in all of the legal rights of society, then argue the case on your own merits. Don't disparage God by dragging Him into the debate. The Mormon Church says it received a "revelation" in 1978 that blacks should be allowed to assume positions of leadership. I think that message had been out there the entire time; it's just some folks down here on earth have a hard time distinguishing the signal from the noise.

Chapter 11: There Is No Santa Claus

In the fall of 1976, I responded to a classified ad from a temp agency seeking department store Santas for the holiday season. I arrived at a strip mall store they rented to fill out an application. I got hired on the spot and then stayed along with another 20 or so newly minted Kris Kringles to participate in a half day of training. It seemed the agency must have been fairly savvy about self-promotion because a reporter from the local paper showed up to cover the event. A quote of mine made it into the article that ran the next day, where I stated something along the lines of being Jewish not an issue because Santa was about making little kids happy. Of course I really meant I was short on cash and happy to find a paying gig.

The modern commercial version of Christmas had been mostly fueled by Jews like songwriter Irving Berlin ("White Christmas") and the Jewish merchants who built up the first generation of big retailers, including Abraham & Strauss, FAO Schwarz, Gimbels, Saks Fifth Avenue and Macy's. And most of the schmaltzy holiday movies were produced by studios run by Jews such as Samuel Goldwyn and Lewis G. Mayer.

Going home with a costume that only fit my 140 lb. frame if I put a pillow under the jacket, I was told to report to Teterboro Airport in North Jersey at 8:00 a.m. on the Friday after Thanksgiving to be flown by helicopter to the parking lot of Brunswick Square Mall, where a huge crowd was expected to be anxiously awaiting Santa's arrival. My dad gave me a lift to the airfield, and the pilot, Jim, was there waiting for me, fueled up and ready to go. It was my first and to this day only helicopter ride I have ever taken. Jim explained that for short trips such as this one, he flew at low altitudes and simply followed the roads below to get to his location, the same as a car would travel. We arrived at the mall in about ten minutes, and as we descended, I was surprised by how few people awaited us. I had been told to expect hundreds of families, and instead, there were just 25 or so people on hand. Stepping out of the chopper and waving to the sparse and shivering crowd, I was driven to the main entrance, where I ascended my throne in the mall's center court.

After dutifully showing up to work for a week and enduring an uncomfortable, heavy outfit with an itchy fake beard while small children laden with all manner of infectious germs scrambled across my lap, the agency called and informed me I had been fired. I asked for a reason. They said I had been terminated because I had arrived an hour early to the big Friday morning helicopter event.

Apparently, there had been a mix-up in communications. The agency had been told to get Santa there at 8:30 a.m. but the mall had advertised the event for 9:30 a.m. An hour after I had touched down, the mall manager had been forced to go out to the parking lot and issue an apology to a throng of disappointed parents and their small children. It had turned into a public relations fiasco and made the manager furious.

"But … but … how could you blame me? Not only had I shown up when I had been instructed to, the helicopter was there waiting for me and the pilot had been given the same schedule. Didn't that prove it wasn't my fault?"

"Oh, by the way," the lady from the agency told me over the phone while she ignored my plea, "they also said you were too skinny."

Chapter 12: You Do Use Your Whole Brain

When I went to school, teachers occasionally said that we only used 80 percent of our brains. They delivered this statement in the tone of an accusation. The implication was that it was their burden to teach lazy students. We kids supposedly didn't use all of our mental faculties, consistent with the same general sloth that led us to not make our beds or turn in our homework. Perhaps what they really meant was that teachers only use 80 percent of *their* brains.

However, modern scientific research has shown that this supposed "fact," like many others from my school days, is false. Science has begun to discover that what we are consciously aware of is only a small part of the total amount of brain activity, like the visual portion of an iceberg. Most cognitive processes, such as hearing, seeing, breathing, and motor coordination, occur at the subconscious level, which is why we can walk and chew gum at the same time. The complexity of the human brain is truly staggering. Some scientists believe there are more neural connections in the human brain—over 100 trillion—than there are stars in the known universe.

Even more amazing is the riddle of consciousness. We can identify many facts about the world, such as the subatomic structure of matter and laws of physics. But there is, as of today, no explanation for how three pounds of wet, gray, organic material produces the sensation that there is a person inside of us with a distinct identity and sense of "me-ness." And while, for example, we can understand the makeup of the electromagnetic spectrum, there is no explanation for why we can look at an object and experience it as the color red or why red-colored lingerie is considered sexy.

It turns out that we use all of our mental capacity. Yet the many varied and wondrous ways in which our brains work, such as the ability of certain people to be able to tell the Kardashians apart, still remain a mystery. But researchers are hard at work on an answer.

Chapter 13: Kid Life Is Better Than Adult Life

When I was a kid, I couldn't wait to get older. Age represented progress. When you are five years old, the thought that you will someday be ten means you can look forward to a time when you will be bigger, stronger, smarter, and more independent. You'll be able to cross the street by yourself, go over to friends' houses whenever you want, ride your bicycle around the neighborhood, and know much more about how the world operates.

And then, when you get to 16 or 17, you'll really be bigger and stronger and smarter. Forget about the bike—you'll drive a car! And at some point, you'll even get laid, the thought of which truly boggles the imagination. (I still believe that my lost virginity was a more significant event in American history than the first man on the moon.)

And when you reach those high school years, college seems like an even greater stage of development. There really will be sex, and lots of it, even if high school was not quite the bacchanal you hoped. (For me, high school was a desert, sexual speaking; there was always an oasis over the next sand dune, but I could never quite reach it.) Suddenly, all those articles about the college hookup scene will seem incredibly tantalizing. And there will be drugs and alcohol. And even better, no parents to harsh your buzz. Okay, you'll have to go to the occasional class and turn in a paper every once in a while, but that doesn't seem all that heavy of a burden, if you take into consideration the non-stop orgy that awaits.

And once you've gotten to college, the next rung on the ladder seems even more enticing—the chance to earn money. You'll get a great job, because after all, you're a smart, special person. Even your mom agrees with that. Once you are on a first name basis with some serious cash, then all kinds of possibilities open up: a great crib, fancy vacations, a new car, and an all-around whirlwind of fun activities.

Unfortunately, after you get out of college, the reality of the cold, cruel world hits you with the force of a karate chop in the solar plexus. The first thing you realize is that adulthood, which seemed like it was full of freedom and excitement, is also very heavy on responsibilities. You've got to pay the bills, and trust me, after more than 30 years of experience at it, they are endless. Then there's all the chores: laundry, groceries, meals for the family, housework, car maintenance, etc.

Life is filled with financial obligations and responsibilities. And much of the labor is tedious and unrewarding, like rooting for the Chicago Cubs.

Then there is the physical decline. As early as your 20s, you begin to realize no matter how hard you partied or energetic you were in your teens, your body has already begun to slow down Just about everyone who turns 30 feels like it's a bit of a joke—*what, me a kid at heart, 30 years old?* But the joke starts to wear thin with the passage of time. Trust me, by 50 you stop laughing.

That is not to say that life is grim and awful. You can still find the journey fulfilling and rewarding—you just need to remember to make sure you get enough fiber in your diet and are under the covers with the lights out by 10 p.m. You need a good night's rest because you've got a lot of bills to pay and chores to attend to tomorrow.

Chapter 14: Most Jobs Are Soul Deadening

As a teenager, I held the position of cashier in a local supermarket. During busy times, incredibly long checkout lines, with waits of over 30 minutes, were common. In those situations, I always felt sorry for the customers. At least I got paid, even if just minimum wage. The supermarket had a couple of baggers—I got promoted from that position myself— but generally most cashiers had to ring up and then bag the merchandise themselves. On occasion, customers frustrated by the long lines, once they got to the register, would position themselves at the end of the conveyer belt and help load in order to speed up the process, a practice that I am still in the habit of to this day.

On one particularly crowded day, I suggested to a person on my line, a woman who appeared to be in her mid-30s, that she could help bag if she wanted to, in order to get out of the store faster. I thought I did her a favor by sharing this information. She did not respond. About 10 minutes after she left, the store manager came over and started yelling at me.

"Don't you ever tell a customer to bag again!" he said, his face twisted with rage.

I wanted to explain that I tried to be helpful but decided not to expend the effort required to explain my actions. I simply assumed that the manager could not be intellectually reasoned with and that the course of least resistance consisted of letting him yell at me as I silently seethed with contempt.

I quit a few weeks later in order to take a summer job as a camp counselor and then applied at another local supermarket when the new school year started. By coincidence, my best friend, Howard, also applied at the same time, and we were both hired together. The store manager told us his preference was not to bring on high school seniors because he wanted to get at least two full years of employment before he had to replace them. We were both juniors, so we met his criteria. However, once work started, I almost immediately regretted my decision. The full-time employees effectively ran an organized theft ring and shoplifted all of their household grocery needs. It appeared they regarded the opportunity to rob the store blind a mere fringe benefit at an establishment with such poor oversight by management. They must have thought to themselves that the steaks were just sitting there, almost asking to be stolen.

Howard had accumulated enough credits to graduate high school early, so he decided to start college in what would have otherwise been his senior year. And I left for a different job at the local drugstore. Again, by coincidence, after a shared first day on the job together, a mere two weeks later, we both resigned at the same time. When we informed the manager of our plans, he erupted in anger, with a degree of outrage that would have been appropriate had we stolen his car, not merely resigned our positions. I endured his tirade with equanimity. Had I cared enough to respond, I would have let him know that Lincoln freed the slaves and we likewise were allowed to leave his employ anytime we pleased.

I was able to get a little bit of karmic justice, as a few months later my mother needed to return a package of cottage cheese that had spoiled. I brought it to the service counter, and the store manager chose not to look up or make eye contact. He silently returned the cash. Call it even. I then took on an alternative minimum wage position in a local pharmacy. This business had better working conditions and coworkers with a higher level of integrity.

A short aside on this point. My high school had a program in which all students, due to overcrowding, participated in a mandatory activity outside of school one day per week, in theory to give them some "community" experience. Several of the options included volunteer work for local nonprofit organizations, but most consisted of slave labor at menial jobs in regular businesses, including, believe or not, being required to pump gas at a service station. I had a friend who did his community service as an indentured servant in the same pharmacy that employed me. He put in a compulsory full day of work for no pay. This took place in the era before bar codes and scanners, so my friend would routinely swipe merchandise that he could readily hide in a jacket pocket, such as cigarettes, candy, and gum. He figured if he got cheated out of a paycheck, he had a license to find a way to generate his own compensation.

In Israel, while I served as a volunteer on a kibbutz, one of the work details assigned to me involved sorting tangerines on a conveyor belt as they went past at a rate of about 10 per second. I had to pull off the bruised pieces of fruit. To my untrained eye, the conveyer belt looked like a blur of orange. I tried to spot the damaged fruit to the best of my rather limited ability. My supervisor came over, looked at the produce I had removed, and started to reprimand me in the same type of moral indignation used by the biblical prophets.

"Why did you remove produce suitable for export? Are you an idiot?" he asked.

I knew enough Hebrew to understand what he said. Determined not to get yelled at further, I gouged each piece of the soft fruit that I pulled off with my thumb, leaving it with a highly visible defect. I finished the rest of the shift bored out of my skull but free of criticism.

In college, I worked for several months in an East Coast chain convenience store that was comparable to a 7-Eleven in size, merchandise, and customer base. The emporium closed at midnight. If you got the closing shift, then you had to complete a number of time-consuming tasks before you could leave the premises: restock the cigarettes behind the counter, clean the deli, shrink-wrap the meats and cheeses, vacuum the store, and throw out the trash. A steady stream of last minute customers, particularly nicotine addicts making one final cigarette run lest they be caught between midnight and daybreak without any smokes, made closing on time a challenge. We couldn't actually lock the door until precisely midnight, and when we did, the store usually contained a couple of customers who still had to be rung up at the register. As a result, I couldn't punch out until a few minutes after the official closing time. I was being paid minimum wage, $3.35 per hour back then, so the additional 4 or 5 minutes on the clock amounted to mere pennies.

After I worked there for a month or so, the assistant manager approached me. She told me that management expected employees to finish the closing shift at midnight. I explained to her the various obstacles that made closing on time impossible.

"Oh, I totally understand," she told me. "It's just that they want you to punch out your time card by twelve."

In a job where I was already paid minimum wage, ownership wanted me to spend a portion of my shift off the clock.

Here's another example of how miserable work can be. My first job out of college, in a Dickensian pension actuarial firm, had a coffee pot in the kitchen. Employees who arrived at the office before the official start time of 8:30 a.m. could help themselves to a free cup of joe. However, the clock in the kitchen was set 10 minutes fast, and I commuted in a carpool that traveled on the traffic-choked Garden State Parkway, which meant I never got to the office early enough for a cup on the house.

I'm sure that these few examples could be multiplied by the millions. Somewhere along the line expect to encounter bad bosses. If that weren't the case, then there would be no hit song entitled, "Take This Job and Shove It."

Chapter 15: There Are No Heroes (Part One)

Jews, despite what seems like an outsized influence on world events, number a mere 14 million. Rounded to the nearest whole number, Jews comprise zero percent of the world's population.

So, even though all the major monotheistic faiths consider the Jewish Bible, or Old Testament, to be part of their Holy Scripture, the various religions approach this document in different ways. For Christianity and Islam, it is preamble to be followed by later works that are also considered to be the Word of God. For us Jews, the Old Testament is all we've got, so we focus on it with greater intensity. And the part we concentrate on the most is the beginning, the first five books, which Jews refer to as the Torah.

The Torah contains all of the great Jewish patriarchs and leaders. These are holy men. Or are they? Consider their track records:

- Adam is given only one commandment to follow, not to eat from the Tree of Knowledge. Lucky enough to live in the Garden of Eden and with only a single law on the books, what does he do but violate it?

- Adam and Eve have two sons, and one of them, Cain, kills his brother Abel. In a world with a total population of four people, they can't find enough elbow room to get out of each other's way, and the first nuclear family in human history contains a murderer.

- Noah is characterized as a "righteous man of his generation." Jewish commentators regard this as a backhanded compliment, meaning for a guy who lived in a time that was so sinful that God destroyed the entire world in a flood, he was merely okay.

- Abraham is willing to sacrifice his son Isaac because he believes that God has commanded him to do so. Today, someone who makes such a claim is regarded as deranged and locked up in a mental institution. Isaac goes mutely along and appears willing to have his throat slit in order to appease an invisible God.

- Joseph's brothers, jealous over the beautiful coat of many colors that their father Jacob gave him, throw

him into a pit and then sell him into
slavery.

For Jews today, many of our prayers start out
with a recitation of our patriarchs, Abraham, Isaac,
and Jacob. As the inheritors of a religion that we
believe commands us toward ethical behavior, we
revere spiritual ancestors who were deeply flawed
individuals, yet contained also greatness within
themselves.

This is not quite the paradox that it seems.
Judaism holds that each individual has two impulses
in perpetual conflict, the inclination to do good, or
the *yetzer hatov*, and the inclination to do evil, the
yetzer hara. While these might seem to be polar
opposites, Jews understand them to be more
interrelated. For example, lust, which Christianity
considers to be on the bad side of the ledger, leads to
procreation, children, and families. Sexual desire,
single-minded as it is, (there is a Yiddish saying: when
the penis stands up, the brains get buried in the
ground), can still lead to positive outcomes. Greed
can motivate entrepreneurs to take great risks and
found successful businesses that lead to economic

51

growth and make all of us better off. And "good" impulses, like study, if pursued too ardently, can cause a person to be removed from the world and indifferent to human concerns.

According to a Jewish anecdote, when a rabbi saw a religious man deep in concentration over his books, ignoring the cries of his young child, he rebuked the man and said, "I don't know what you think you are studying, but whatever it is, if it causes you to ignore a crying child, then it isn't Torah."

So we're all flawed. Even the heroes we worship.

Chapter 16: There Are No Heroes (Part Two)

Just like the biblical patriarchs, America has its own set of heroes, the fathers of our country, such as George Washington and Thomas Jefferson. They were men who fought for freedom, and their words have inspired us for generations: "We hold these truths to be self-evident, that all men are created equal," and "Give me liberty or give me death."

These are inspirational words indeed, unless you happened to have been either a slave or a woman. For those same great heroes were more or less resigned to the idea that "men" meant white men only. The Founding Fathers not only accommodated slavery, but in many cases, such as Washington and Jefferson, were slave owners themselves. And Jefferson almost certainly engaged in sex with at least one of his slaves, a relationship which is difficult to view as consensual, given the circumstances. And in regard to women, the Founding Fathers forged a nation dedicated to the cause of liberty, albeit one in which the ladies were not allowed to vote.

Today, it is somewhat common, to the point of political correctness, to regard traditions and practices as having some type of inherent validity simply because they exist. This has led to the belief that moral relativism has devalued ethical standards and put all cultures on an equal footing. If one society tolerates country clubs that don't admit female members, while another mutilates the genitals of young girls, they are not the same. There is a reason why the criminal code distinguishes between felonies and misdemeanors. Not all wrongs are equal. But that shouldn't blind us to the flaws of the great white men in our history books. Maybe a fuller understanding of history will give us greater tolerance for the shortcomings of the leaders of today. Yes, Bill Clinton had a tryst with an intern that had more detail than could be stomached over breakfast. *The cigar went where?* But he also presided over a robust economy. Let's just not try to make anyone into a hero, or at least reserve that category for people who really deserve it.

Chapter 17: Math Is a Big Waste of Time

One of the worst things that happens to kids in middle school and continues in high school and college is being forced to study upper-level math. Basic computation, the ability to add, subtract, multiply, and divide is a useful skill, as is a sense of the relative size of numbers. So I'm not against the teaching of arithmetic, one of the crucial three "r's" of grade school.

Companies have long employed trick questions in their interviews, not to see if candidates know the right answer, but more as a window into their problem-solving skills. Google has gotten a lot of notoriety regarding how you would save yourself if you shrank to the size of a dime but still had the same density and found yourself trapped inside a blender. First, you have to put aside the obvious flaw that if you lived in a world in which people randomly shrank to the size of pocket change and found their lives in peril as a result, Google's business model might no longer be relevant. However, the correct answer is that since your density hasn't changed, you still weigh as much as you did before you found yourself miniaturized, and your muscles would be incredibly powerful, meaning you could jump right out before you were julienned by the razor-sharp blades.

A couple of questions that are less silly include trying to guess how many miles of track there are on the New York City subway system or how many gas stations there are in the United States. I actually asked the former question once while interviewing a job candidate for an entry-level position, and her response was, "I don't know," thereby bringing the entire exercise in logical thinking to a screeching halt.

But here's how you might answer this, or at least think about a credible response. Consider that it's common knowledge that New York is one of the biggest cities in the world, or at least was until it was dwarfed by former also-rans such as Karachi (13 million), Tianjan (11 million), and Shenzen (10 million), as quick Internet search shows. The world is so mixed-up these days that New York no longer even makes the top 20. But as a significant metropolis, you would figure that the built-up urban area probably extends about 5-10 miles from the city center. Also, it would be reasonable to expect that a subway system would have multiple lines that stretch in different directions. Even if you knew nothing about New York's mass transportation, a reasonable guess would be 10–15 lines, each one about 10–15 miles in length. A logical thinking person would then conclude that New York has somewhere around 100–225 miles of subway tracks and might guess somewhere in the middle, say around 150–175. And that wouldn't be a bad conjecture. The correct answer, 209 miles of routes, is discoverable at the click of a mouse, since we can't shrink to the size of a dime and put in a blender. Google can let you find this kind of information without even moving from your chair.

That's the kind of math you need to know to navigate in this world. Why do you need to learn algebra, trigonometry, calculus, or any of the other mathematical concepts that you are ceaselessly bludgeoned with, starting in those unfortunate middle school years?

The short answer is that you don't. Every year,

the United States produces about 1.6 million college graduates. The number of college students who major in math is tiny—a mere 16,000—fewer than one percent. At the master's degree level, about 700,000 degrees in all disciplines are awarded annually, of which a mere 5,000 are in math. And at the graduate level, you can fit all the annual recipients of math degrees into a single high school gym. Out of 150,000 total doctorate degrees awarded each year, a puny 1,500 are in math.[10]

This state of affairs would almost be funny if it wasn't tragic. No one, roughly speaking, specializes in math as an adult, yet we all have it stuffed into us until it comes out of our ears as middle and high school students.

There is a two-fold reason why math is mandatory for everyone, regardless of need. The first is that the American educational system is remarkably impervious to change. As noted previously, we still close schools down for the summer, even though the majority of kids have not been needed to help harvest the crops for over a century. The second is that the Russians launched

Sputnik in 1957, taking an early lead in the space race, and America was desperate to catch up. We responded with JFK pledging to put a man (not a woman) on the moon by the end of the decade. A ripple effect was an increase in the amount of math and science in the standard school curriculum. We needed to catch up with the Commies! A sad consequence is the math that less than 1 percent of us will pursue later in life is forced down the throats of the other 99-plus percent.

There is a counterargument, which is that even if math beyond grade school level is of little relevance to most peoples' adult lives, it still is worthwhile as a way to sharpen your brain. That may be true, but there are only 24 hours in a day. We live in a world of finite resources. While math is worthwhile, so is music, art, the humanities, and just plain having fun. Consider trigonometry, which is a branch of mathematics that is primarily involved with the various relationships between the sides and angles of a triangle. Its primary application is navigation. When was the last time you ever had to navigate a ship by hand?

And they even managed to screw up simple arithmetic when I was a kid. I got exposed to one of the most inane educational fads to get inflicted upon a generation of students—so-called "new math." You would think that nothing could be more basic than the times table, and only a complete confederation of dunces could screw it up. You would be correct, and those dunces were the people who ran public schools and decided that math could be "improved."

What I mostly remember about math from my grade school years is my poor performance in the subject. For example, the universally accepted framework of counting across all cultures is base-10. You'll note that this rather conveniently corresponds to the number of fingers on both hands. One doesn't have to be an evolutionary biologist to understand that the human brain and the human hand developed in an interdependent way. Certainly, we all know that our wonderful opposable thumbs (I once had a teacher with thumbs the size of 40-watt light bulbs), which give us an ability unparalleled in the rest of the animal world to grasp objects and manipulate tools, were integral to the development of human intelligence. You can thank some anonymous long-age ancestor on our hominid family tree for trying to pick up a dung beetle with two sticks, which unbeknownst to him triggered a set of evolutionary changes that eventually led to *Duck Dynasty*.

Even today, with calculators and spreadsheets, counting on one's fingers can come in handy (no pun intended). It is as natural for us to count using a base-10 system as it is to use our eyes to see. Despite that, one of the pointless tasks I and my peers were forced to persevere through was how to count in base-8. The idea was to get us to grasp the essence of a "base" system, since base-10 comes so intuitively to us. But this is like asking children to learn to navigate by sonar like bats, so that we can understand how alternative forms of visual systems can work. It wasn't until later, in higher grades, that I realized I was actually good at math—the real kind, that is.

But even though I was relatively proficient at math, the level of abstraction at the middle and high school level is a complete and utter waste for the overwhelming majority of us who do not go on to study the discipline at the college and graduate school level.

The importance of being able to understand arithmetic is obvious, since money is an integral part of our lives and the knowledge of how to budget is a valuable skill. But who needs to master, for example, the quadratic formula, the binomial theorem or linear equations? Yet these concepts, and many others, are considered information that every high school student in the United States should have to know in order to receive their diploma. If the reason why seems unclear, remember, it's because of Sputnik: The Russians are coming!

Chapter 18: Men Are Dumb But Have the Advantage

Anyone with half a brain in their head—almost the standard definition of a male, as it happens—can see that women are smarter than men. While the general belief is that women are more emotional—after all, they are the ones with mysterious "cycles" that affect their moods—it is men who allow feelings to overpower logic. Given the ease with which men get aroused, that means that almost no male under the age of 30 should be allowed to make any significant life decisions (except for getting married).

Men also are more prone to anger and are competitive to the point of destructiveness. A man will run a company into the ground in order to try to become the biggest competitor in an industry. A woman will ask whether the growth comes along with extra profits that make it worthwhile.

Women are also better at building consensus and helping make sure that people feel a sense of buy-in. And they are cleaner, dress nicer, and smell better.

There is a saying (misguided) feminists use that

"women need a man the way that a fish needs a bicycle" to discredit the idea that a committed relationship is a necessary part of any woman's life. I refer to this philosophy as misguided only because in my own case I see how a long marriage to me has been a continuous source of mirth for Mrs. Harris, as I stumble from one fiasco to another. It's reached a point where she fears that I may electrocute myself if I attempt to change a light bulb.

And yet, men are the ones that have the advantage in life. I don't mean an advantage that is derived from the kind of old-fashioned laws that discriminate against women, which a generation burned their bras in protest against. Without legal authority, isn't any advantage of men a paradox, given our inferiority? Not as much as you might think. An empty brain can be a surprising advantage.

Spend enough time in a loving, committed relationship, and you will discover that your female partner (I know nothing of the dynamics of gay relationships) remembers with total recall every slight injustice that ever transpired. Remember that time you reached for the ketchup bottle first before offering her any at dinner in a restaurant 27 years ago? Of course not. You don't even remember the meal taking place. But it has been seared into the consciousness of your beloved. Every move you made or didn't make, every single conversation, every chance remark, has been stored away and can be retrieved with perfect recall.

Consider as further proof a classic Jerry Seinfeld joke. "Women," he says, "always want to know what's on men's minds. The answer," he tells us, "is nothing. We just stand around without thinking about anything at all."

My contention is the more you forget, the happier you are. Around the world, nations have engaged in senseless conflicts because of ancient grudges. Someone stole someone else's sand dune or herd of goats and the next 50 generations kept fighting over it. To forget about the conflict makes much more sense. Men are good—no, make that great—forgetters. Your wife threw a plate at your head for suggesting that a particular cut of jeans might not work as well on her figure as it once did. By the next time you have a romantic encounter with her, sweeping up the pieces of broken crockery seems as long ago as the NY Jets winning a Super Bowl.

Your significant other will get upset with you for your lapses in memory. But by the next day, you'll have forgotten that she was even mad.

Advantage, men.

Chapter 19: The Government Is Out to Get You

No, I haven't bought into any of the wacky conspiracy theories out there, like the unmarked black UN surveillance helicopters flying around the neighborhood. (Although I did see one land in a neighbor's backyard, and the next thing you know, the house had a "for sale" sign in front of it.) And I also don't mean the tremendous inequities in our criminal justice system, where people living in poor neighborhoods have their front doors smashed in with battering rams as SWAT teams search for drugs, while in the wealthy suburbs, we all get nicely stoned in the privacy of our homes.

What I am referring to is the dirty little secret known as the Body Mass Index, or BMI, which is promoted as a measure of healthy weight. While it seems harmless enough to encourage Americans to forgo a third helping of Chunky Monkey, the war against fat is used as a tool of oppression, as hardly a day goes by without some mention in the news about America's obesity problem. Why, even Michelle

Obama, with the most buff pair of First-Lady arms in American history, grows vegetables at the White House and emphasizes healthy eating habits.

The US Department of Health and Human Services has a BMI calculator on their website. The categories are simple enough:

Underweight: Under 18.5
Normal: 18.5 to 24.9
Overweight: 25.0 to 29.9
Obese: Over 30

First of all, take note of how incredibly patronizing such terminology is. I mean, really, "overweight" and "obese" as labels for actual human beings? It's like a school nurse coming in at assembly and telling all the fat kids to get up and sit in the first three rows. And could you be any more judgmental than by the use of a term like "normal"? If the majority of the population doesn't fall in that category, then shouldn't it be the other way around? If most people are classified as overweight and obese, then why would you term a minority normal? It would be like a survey of America's hall closets, which considers normal only those that resemble the "after" photo of a closet-cleaning business. My closets have a jumble of shoes on the floor, and I bet if you were honest, you'd admit that yours do too.

To begin with, we need new terminology. I suggest we replace "underweight" with "unhealthy," and then bump "normal" and "overweight" up, pushing "obese" right off the chart. That seems reasonable. People who no longer resemble their high school yearbook photos should not receive a scarlet badge of shame.

But for me, it's personal. You see, I have taken off about 20 pounds ever since my father, at dinner in Florida one night about 10 years ago, was kind enough to tell me that I wasn't "putting on weight" as I had commented, but rather that I had "put on weight." In the ensuing decade, I have gone from paunchy, though mostly hidden by the forgiving nature of male clothing, to a physique that is considerably more fit and trim. Unclothed, it's a different story: I am still a squat, hairy beast, hideous to behold. But, fully dressed, my approximately 165 pounds on a medium-sized frame is, everything else taken into consideration, not bad for a man my age.

This would all be fine except for one small problem: I am quite bow-legged, to the extent that once, while a teen and clad in short pants, I was asked by an older woman if I had rickets as a child. I measure out at 5 feet, 8 $\frac{1}{2}$ inches, a misleading statistic, like the average amount of annual precipitation in Seattle, which is lower than New York, even though it rains in Seattle far more often. We don't have the summer thunderstorms hotter, more humid climates endure, hence the statistical oddity of Seattle's total annual precipitation. The reality is if the curvature of my leg bones could somehow be magically straightened, I might stand as tall as 5 feet, 10 inches.

My weight generally fluctuates around 165–167 pounds. At the high end of that range and using my (misleading) measured height, I score 25.0 on the BMI, lumped in with the fat kids by a mere $\frac{1}{10}$ of a percentage point. If only I had been blessed with straight legs, my BMI would practically qualify me for the catwalk.

Since President Obama has ceded our

sovereignty to the UN, there isn't much we can do about the unmarked black helicopters. But, if we resolve to generate a storm of protest, I'm sure we can overhaul the BMI index.

Chapter 20: We're All Gay Now

I started junior high school as a scrawny, pimply youth with crooked teeth, thereby resembling most of my peers. If you really wanted to hurt my feelings, you simply could have said, "Hey, Harris, go look in a mirror!" Had I dared to do so with a genuinely open mind, the awful reflection that would have greeted me would have been sufficient insult to put me in my place.

But instead of taking the handiest ammunition, the mockery which typically sprang to our male adolescent lips was "fag," short for faggot or homosexual. I'm not even sure I knew the term in grade school, but I certainly learned its meaning by the end of the first day of junior high. We uttered it as easily as we breathed. I'm sure that I was called a fag and referred to others by the same term at least ten times a day for several years running.

Part of being a fag was constant ridicule for the presumed performance of fellatio. Interestingly, no one was ever castigated for being on the receiving end of oral sex. In this hypothetical world teeming with gays, we never envisioned who possessed the organ being fellated. And that a girl could perform such an act was beyond the capacity for our just-barely adolescent minds, as if the ancient Stone Age shepherds had be given an opportunity to look through the Hubble telescope.

I recall the first time I saw a pornographic picture in seventh grade. It was in the boys' bathroom—how stereotypical can you get? It was a single photograph, which showed about 20 unclothed people engaged in various forms of sexual activity. It took me about half a minute to figure out exactly what this photo journalism consisted of. Like a jigsaw puzzle that finally begins to form an identifiable image, I suddenly realized, *Holy shit, those guys have stuck their wieners into every imaginable female orifice*. I don't recall if I even felt a tiny rumble of sexual excitement. It was more like the preparation for your driver's test in order to demonstrate a certain level of knowledge of an adult behavior. *Oh, so that's what it looks like*.

Since we kids back then knew very little about sex, we certainly did not realize the full diversity of behaviors it could take. For us, being a faggot meant you gave head to other males. We lacked the knowledge of alternative forms of gay sexual activity or the fact that sex of any type strengthened the emotional bond between two people who love one another.

Gay was anything outside of the mainstream, like a lack of interest sports. I was a rabid sports fan. My adolescence coincided neatly with the relatively brief golden era in the New York Knicks' team history when they won two championships in 1970 and again in 1973. (The 7th and deciding game of the 1970 final round series against the Lakers aired on television the Friday night of my Bar Mitzvah weekend. I can still feel the sting of disappointment that I missed the greatest game the team ever played.)

Back in my youth, to be a faggot meant "not part of the majority," like other boys who rooted for sports teams at a time when society was a lot more homogenous. Today, America is a land of individualists. People form start-up companies and work from their homes. We drink beer made by microbreweries with whimsical names like New

England Ghandi-Bot and Polygamy Porter. Some men wear kilts. I have seen this myself in Seattle. Others write blogs, self-publish books, sell their art online, and follow music of every type, such as Techno Country and Hip House. Male behaviors that used to be automatic, like ownership of a TV, a subscription to the local paper, or an interest in sports, have eroded sharply in popularity. When I was a kid, I didn't know any other boys who failed to follow sports faithfully. Today that is no longer the case. My youngest son, age 15, is a highly accomplished dancer. Dance is a sport that, based on a particular studio, is either 100 percent girls, or as is the case where he dances, only 95 percent female. He looks good—no, make that great— in ballet tights. He is muscular, athletic, and ripped. Had I known him when I was the same age, I would have termed him a fag in a heartbeat. Funny thing is he's already on his third or fourth girlfriend, at least the ones my wife and I know about. Somehow, a great dancer with rock-hard core appeals to the young ladies. Go figure.

My middle son conforms to stereotypes, as he is in fact a fag . . . er . . . I mean, he's gay. He doesn't have the slightest interest in team sports, although he does practice yoga, jogs regularly, and is otherwise relatively physically fit.

My daughter also has zero interest in sports, but she's a girl, so it doesn't matter. She does think Eli Manning is quite hot. I explained to her that he's married (as is she) but again, since I don't understand girls, I'm not sure what the purpose of celebrity crushes are for. All I know is that a lack of interest in sports is no longer a sign of same sex-orientation. And to be gay is no longer odd, because we're all gay now.

What would a man with my figure look like in a kilt?

Chapter 21: Count on Some Good Luck

I once read a story about a math professor who had an interesting tactic for instruction on the subject of probability. He would give his freshman introductory statistics class, with over 100 students, a take-home exercise. Half the students received a blank score sheet with instructions to flip a coin a hundred times and accurately record the results. The other half of the class got the same score sheet but were told to make up phony results.

The next day, the professor collected and rapidly eyeballed each of the sheets and was able to tell with stunning accuracy which of the students had actually flipped a coin and which had submitted fictitious answers. The trick was that the students who made up the results seriously underestimated the odds of multiple heads or tails in a row. While the probability of consecutive heads or tails for a handful of tosses is low, it isn't astronomical. The expected outcome of either 5 consecutive heads or 5 consecutive tails out of 100 attempts is 94 percent. (The math is a bit tedious, so trust me on this one.) If the professor

77

didn't see 5 consecutive heads or tails, he assumed that he had the fake sheets, since he correctly imagined that students who made up the results would be reluctant to enter something that appeared to have a low probability. But even things that are unlikely still happen if the sample size is large enough.

The reason for this digression into flipping coins is to illustrate a larger point, which is that what seems unlikely in a single moment often may actually be extremely probable when viewed over a larger time frame. I know it may seem counterintuitive, since as a culture we place so much value on hard work and initiative, but to hope for good luck is not as misplaced an idea as it first seems.

In the business world, luck sometimes takes the form of just being in the right place at the right time. When I moved to Seattle in 1990, Microsoft was just in the early stages of a remarkable 20-year run, in which it probably created more widely distributed wealth than any single company in the history of business. To put the financial phenomenon of Microsoft into context, consider that Bill Gates has given away two-thirds of his fortune, and he *still* is the richest guy in the world. For many years, Microsoft had a policy of giving every employee stock options, from the mailroom clerks on up. Over the last five to ten years, as Microsoft's founding leaders, including Bill, left for greener pastures, the company has become far more conventional. Their stock has been dead in the water since the end of the dotcom bubble, and they've even had layoffs at underperforming business units, something that would have once been unthinkable.

But for a very long and very magical time, regardless of your role at Microsoft, from high-ranking executives who traveled in the comfort of business class and lodged at five-star hotels all the way down to the lowest paid of individual contributors, you got your own personal piece of the gravy train. And if you joined the organization early enough, even if you were at the bottom of the totem pole, you still got rich, as in the "filthy" type. Year after year, Microsoft would create another couple of hundred millionaires. There was even a motto inside the company, "rest and vest," which meant if you weren't particularly ambitious and didn't aspire to a senior level position, you would just do your job adequately, wait the four and a half years until your stock vested, and then figure out whether going to work every day was still meaningful.

I had a friend who was on the staff of an Internet start-up that went belly up in the dotcom bust. (In cruder times, when I worked on Wall Street, I would have said they went "tits up" but that is a very vulgar expression. I am now a more refined person.) She joined Microsoft soon afterward. Microsoft was beginning to transition from a dream factory where everyone became as wealthy as Croesus to just another big company where regular working stiffs hoped they would get a good annual performance review and hang onto their job. There still were many people there from the glory days, sitting on immense fortunes but accustomed to work they didn't need. She said that internally they were known as "volunteers."

Luck happens to take a lot of different forms, not just the business variety. Maybe it's to find the right person to marry or to have the universe answer one of your prayers and deliver you a child.

And in regard to luck, it's also a good idea to be careful not to confuse good fortune with special abilities. For 20 years I worked in the technology sector in Seattle. I had the opportunity to meet many people who left Microsoft and were determined to make their mark on the world with an exciting start-up that was destined for success. Wasn't that what they were all about? All they had to do was take one look at their brokerage statement to confirm their business acumen.

Yet, what is striking is how few of the many ex-Microsoft entrepreneurs were able to replicate that magic anywhere else. To be fair, the odds that someone will launch a successful start-up are daunting. If it was easy, then everyone would do it. But you'd think by now there would be a couple of dozen dynamic young companies with innovative business models generated by former Microsofties, when in fact, depending on how you define success, the number is closer to zero. Probably the most significant of the lot is Intellectual Ventures, founded by Microsoft's former Chief Technology Officer,

Nathan Myhrvold. His company, which buys up patents to collect licensing revenues, is successful, in a financial sense but not regarded as an innovator on the order of Facebook or Google.

This is not to say that people from Microsoft weren't smart—many of them were, and undoubtedly there were at least a few that were brilliant. But the criticism of Microsoft for years was that their success was built upon acquired technology. They were relentless at selling, but unlike, say Apple, some critics insisted they never developed anything internally that could be regarded as a breakthrough.

But the people who worked there were lucky. Right now my strategy for funding my kids' college education is to get a bit lucky myself. Seems like the most sensible option available under the circumstances.

Chapter 22: Getting Old Stinks

When I was younger, I thought that older people were similar versions of my youthful self who just happened to have lived longer. And then, in no particular order, the following indignities were inflicted upon me:

- I put on weight.

- I became bald.

- My gums began to recede, which required regular flossing to maintain good oral hygiene.

- Hair began to grow on my ears. (If you think that's disgusting to read, just imagine how disgusting it is to be the person it happens to.)

- I no longer care about whether I impressed people or not and have become insufferably boring.

- There is no fooling young people, including my kids. They can immediately sense that I am old.

- I have reached an age where I now need to have colonoscopies for the rest of my life. (Insert favorite colonoscopy joke here.)

The only offsetting benefit is that there are some people who refuse to grow old gracefully. I am so grateful for the Donald Trumps and Joan Rivers of the world, who resort to comb-overs and facelifts that defy nature, which allows the rest of us to sit on our couches and derive entertainment from their desire to look more youthful than their birth certificates would otherwise justify. Although, I have to say, it's no fun to be bald. Maybe "The Donald" is onto something.

Chapter 23: Anything Is Possible

It may be hard to believe, given the freewheeling times we live in, but once American society was incredibly prudish. My wife moved here from Amsterdam in 1978 immediately after we got married. Back then, Holland was a completely hedonistic society with legalized pot and prostitution and a generous welfare system.

America at that time, by contrast, was in a state of denial over the fact that human beings, when unclothed, do not possess the smooth plastic private parts of Barbie dolls. One of the first things my better half noted in her new country was that Playtex bra commercials on television showed the models with the underwear *over* sweaters.

Fast forward to 2014, and one of the most popular retailers in malls is Victoria's Secret. Sexy lingerie is provocatively displayed in my hometown across from the wholesomeness of the Hello Kitty store. No topic is off-limits in our society, from anti-gay Republicans picking up men in airport restrooms to a heterosexual politician texting photographs of his package to female admirers.

A reflection of our new more permissive attitude is that one of the most noteworthy theatrical productions of the last few years is *The Vagina Monologues*. Unless you've been living in one cave over from the top brass of Al-Qaeda and haven't kept up with the news, you probably are aware that this is a production in which women talk about their . . . um . . . you know. And, perhaps the most amazing thing is that I have yet to see it. Maybe I'll surprise my wife with tickets for Mother's Day.

Chapter 24: The Flesh Is Willing

When you are young, life abounds with temptation. In school, if you were an easily aroused lad like me, there were many times you had difficulty listening to the teacher drone on about the main crops of Colonial America (peaches, walnuts and fennel, if memory serves me correctly) while surrounded by so much delectable female temptation. Yes, the hypotenuse of a triangle has some useful function, I'm sure; maybe it helps fold the laundry or check your car's engine oil. But I was concerned about a different type of geometry, the golden ratio of the female form. Now that was a fascinating math concept.

But the problem with those adolescent years was that I had, to put it in modern parlance, no "game." I would have gladly engaged in libidinous pleasure-seeking sessions if I could have found someone to join me. But girls back then protected their virtue, at least when I was in the vicinity. I recall the time I asked one particularly shapely lass to slow dance at a junior high school dance.

"I can't," she replied, "my side hurts." Yet, less than five minutes later, I saw her in the arms of a rival for her affection, a boy who had nothing over me except better looks, less acne, and a more chiseled musculature.

Today, the youth who stole what should have been my place on the dance floor, might, for all I know, be a grease monkey at a Midas Muffler shop. He might also, however, own 50 Midas shops across a multistate area and live in greater style than I do. I prefer to believe the former.

As you get older, you usually discover that regardless of where you started, you do in fact develop a way to interrelate with the opposite gender that does not invoke nausea or cause them to erupt in howls of laughter. And you enter into a life that includes sexual activity, with another person, that is. But many times, when you want to get in the mood, you start to think about the need to wake up early the next morning to go to work, or even worse, the inability to sleep through the night because of crying kids. The hedonistic lifestyle you could have pursued, for most of us, gets replaced by the dull thrum of ordinary monogamy. But that ordinary existence is punctuated by moments of excitement, such as lights out early on school nights.

Chapter 25: There Is Life after High School

This is a concept that seems hard to wrap one's head around because so much of life seems defined by our high school experiences. We all know who was good-looking, who was popular, who came from a rich family, and who was into drugs. Just for the record, I smoked a lot of weed in high school and lacked any desirable personal characteristics, making my social life bleak, which the effects of the pot at least partially offset. And even the use of reefer was a sort of loserish thing to do, as the cool kids got drunk. Booze was where it was at socially.

I have a problem in this regard: I simply cannot hold my liquor. I have been drunk about seven or eight times in my life, and most of those incidents ended in a stomach-churning manner. In fact, my wife, who I rely on to help review my books in draft form, has told me that she can't take any more of the stories of my inebriated escapades, like the time I . . . uh oh, I'd better withhold any details if I want to avoid being told to sleep in a tent in the backyard.

I'm not sure the popular kids, the boys who were good at sports and the girls who were just plain good-looking, have had any happier adult lives than those of us who trudged through the school corridors more anonymously. But they were more popular back then, and I wonder sometimes if that counts extra.

Despite the seemingly long odds, I was able to put myself on a path to eventual happiness. I got married, had kids, enjoyed a fair bit of professional success, and even had some real adventures. I suppose all of us former nerds have the same fantasy regarding high school, where we become famous and then return to our hometown to deliver a speech at a graduation ceremony as a distinguished alumnus, celebrated, applauded, cheered. We'll recognize many of the parents in the audience, those who remained in the local community, eventually seeing their own kids attend the same institution. Finally, a chance to settle old scores and revisit long-held grudges presents itself.

I suspect most of us were very different from our adult selves in high school. For example, according to

David Maraniss, author of *Barack Obama: The Story*, even our current president was a stoner in high school. Maraniss claims that Obama's exploits included being known as a member of the "Choom Gang," with choom being local slang for smoking pot, and was an advocate of a technique called "total absorption" where marijuana was consumed in a sealed car with the all the windows tightly closed.[11]

If I became president, I could just imagine myself invited back to speak at my local high school and elated to be able to gloat over the turn in fortunes since graduation. I probably would use the bully pulpit to settle old scores. Who knows, I might even throw my weight around as commander-in-chief.

Fortunately, most of our fantasies go unrealized. Let's just say it's probably all for the best that my business address isn't 1600 Pennsylvania Avenue.

Chapter 26: Social Science Is Intellectually Flabby

You know all those studies that you see quoted in the news on practically a daily basis, such as TV causes violence, listening to Mozart makes you smarter, or going to college leads to lifelong higher earnings? Well, unfortunately, the foundation that this type of research stands upon is flawed, and many findings of this type are questionable.

Some of the cause-and-effect relationships that we routinely take for granted are either overstated or only correlated with other factors, such as the claim that going to college leads to more money down the road. Young people who go to college, as a group, generally are smarter, possess a stronger work ethic, and have families with greater financial resources than the kids who don't. College helps, but so does the discipline to focus on long-term goals and to grow up in a stable home.

How we turn out as individuals is a combination of two factors: our inherited genetic makeup and our environment, or as it is sometimes referred to, nature vs. nurture.

For a long time, it was thought to be difficult to separate these two because they are so intertwined. Most children inherit both their DNA and their home environment from their parents, although this is not always the case, given adoption.

If parents who love of skiing raise their children to be good skiers, which was more significant in the development of that talent, nature or nurture? Although that question had long been challenging to answer, recent research on identical twins has shed exciting new light on this topic. Identical twins are genetically the same. While people often fear the idea of cloning, clones already exist—we just call them twins. But since most twins are raised in the same family, you still face the issue of teasing out the impact of environment vs. inherited characteristics.

While the majority of identical twins are indeed raised in the same household, not all are. A fascinating study on this topic was conducted by Minnesota Center for Twin and Adoption Research at the University of Minnesota. In 1979, researcher Thomas Bouchard came across a pair of identical twins separated at birth, reared apart, and then reunited at age 39. When they found one another, they discovered the following similarities in their lives:

- They both married women named Linda, got divorced, and then both remarried women named Betty.

- One had a son named James Allan and the other had a son named James Alan.

- They both named their dogs Toy.

- Each vacationed in Florida within the same three-block area.

- Both had some law enforcement training and had been part-time deputy sheriffs in Ohio.

- Each smoked Salem's and drank Miller Lite.

While the similarities between these two twins seem remarkable, they are not unique. The University of Minnesota and other researchers have identified many twins separated at birth and later reunited. Findings about the similarities of separated identical twins have proven to be consistent and striking.

The twin studies support the notion that certain traits, such as intelligence, academic achievement, and measures of personality, are significantly dependent upon the genes one inherits from parents. This does not mean that biology is destiny—many tall people give birth to short children and vice versa. But according to neuroscientist Steven Pinker, in *The Blank Slate: The Modern Denial of Human Nature,* the scientific community has reached a general consensus that genes play a significant role in shaping characteristics such as IQ or degree of introversion/extroversion. The idea that humans are a "blank slate," Pinker argues, has been overturned, and the debate now centers around the degree to which intelligence is heritable, with estimates ranging from 50-70 percent.[12]

This is the fact that calls into question most social science research. Consider the widely held belief that exposure to Mozart as a baby will make you smarter.

In 1998, Zell Miller, the governor of Georgia, proposed that the parents of every child born in the state be sent a Mozart CD on the theory it would assist their intellectual development.

Putting aside the validity of the assumption, which has not been demonstrated, it's easy to see why one would choose to believe it. Classical music is somewhat of an acquired taste, and my guess is it positively correlates with wealth and income. And wealth and income positively correlate with intelligence. Our society is largely a meritocracy, and while there are many paths to success, intelligence is one of the most common.

So when you see studies that demonstrate linkages between various child-rearing techniques and outcomes, you have no idea whether the results are attributable to good genes or a good upbringing. While the children of good athletes may benefit from the training they receive from one or both of their parents, they may also be the fortunate beneficiaries of DNA for superior athletic ability.

That doesn't mean how you parent is inignificant. Everyone wants to be loved and taken care of, and every person deserves a happy childhood. But you have no idea how your kids are going to turn out, and there is little you can do to change the outcome. Don't love them because you hope to turn them into clones of yourself (or fans of Mozart). Love them because they are your kids. That should be reason enough.

Chapter 27: I Wish Democrats Were Smarter

Life is filled with problems. As Job (that's the biblical Job, not Steve Jobs) said, "Man is born to trouble as the sparks fly upward." Our society has too much crime, too much poverty, too much injustice. The question is how to make things better, especially without inadvertently making them worse.

When it comes to the economy, it's obvious that one of our primary goals should be to end poverty and raise everyone's standard of living to at least a level of modest comfort. This would mean that all of us would have access to adequate food, decent housing, be well-clothed, and receive affordable health care.

Since government, in theory, has the potential to make things better, the temptation to pass laws that direct the economy to behave in a certain fashion can be overwhelming. This line of thinking suggests if you want people to make more money, then an appropriate step would be to raise the minimum wage. Unfortunately, this also raises labor costs for businesses, which slows down overall hiring. Good intention, bad outcome.

If you'd like cars to be safer, you can force automakers to add exceedingly powerful airbags that operate independently of seatbelts, which means they can and do decapitate children and small adults, another case of well-intentioned people who implement ill-advised rules. More stringent building requirements lead to higher housing costs. Opposing education vouchers, in order to protect unionized teaching jobs, means more poor kids trapped in bad schools. High taxes discourage investment. Opposing free trade raises costs for American consumers and leads to inflation. A few more bad ideas: high-speed trains to nowhere, subsidized ethanol, subsidized wind power, subsidized solar power, subsidized . . . well, you get the picture.

Good intentions do not good policy make. And that is why I wish Democrats had a better understanding of how to manage the economy.

Chapter 28: I Wish Republicans Were More Enlightened

When it comes to economic policy, the Republican tendency to favor lighter regulation, and free markets is smarter than the Democrat's approach of using the heavy hand of government to inadvertently screw things up. Based on this fact, you might think that Republicans are smarter than Democrats. Sadly you would be mistaken because when it comes to social policies, Republicans are, unfortunately, perpetually a generation behind the times. I say "unfortunately" because I wish I could vote Republican, but I just can't bring myself to do so. I would be better off financially and so would almost everyone else. But, to quote a certain Jewish carpenter, "For what shall it profit a man, if he shall gain the whole world and lose his own soul?" While Jesus was talking about the kingdom of heaven, as a Jew I am focused on the here and now of life on earth. My goal is to see society become more free and just, and Republicans, at least at the national level of government, are a major impediment to the

101

realization of that vision.

The concept of freedom is relatively consistent across time. What has changed is society's view of who deserves to be part of what is known as "the circle of freedom." Originally, in America, entry into the circle of freedom was limited to property-owning white males. Gradually, all white males were allowed to enter. Then came feminism and the Civil Rights movements, and barriers to African-Americans and women began to drop away. More recently, gays have been allowed to enter the circle. The last remaining group still on the outside looking in is illegal immigrants.

Through all of this, Republicans have been dragged kicking and screaming into the modern era. In every case, conservatives fought against the very principles they supposedly stood for, a free society where all citizens enjoy the same rights. Fortunately, once society accepts a formerly oppressed minority into the circle, there appears to be no turning back the clock.

The group currently on the margin, illegal immigrants and especially their children, is worthy of some discussion. Immigrants, predominately from Latin America, have come to the United States mostly for financial reasons, to work and be able to improve the standard of living for themselves and their families. Economists generally disagree on many issues, but the impact of immigration on the US economy is not one of them. We benefit enormously from the influx of cheap labor. The argument that illegals take jobs away from Americans is not supported by the facts. Illegals tend to dominate in industries such as agriculture and slaughterhouses, jobs that are dangerous, physically demanding, poorly paid, and in remote locations.

The flow of undocumented labor could be dramatically minimized if the United States liberalized its immigration laws. But here Republicans are their own worst enemy. Party leadership realizes that some segments of the business community, in particular farmers, are reliant upon illegal immigrants for their very survival. And technology companies and venture capitalists constantly lobby for the United States to open its borders and allow in more highly skilled workers.

Technology, in particular, is an industry where talent is paramount. Silicon Valley would be unrecognizable without immigrants or the children of immigrants who have built leading companies such as Intel and Google.

But Republicans appear hamstrung by the demographics of the voters they predominately appeal to, religious and social conservatives. Unfortunately, they are stuck at an ideological crossroads. Illegal immigrants committed a crime, and no matter how shortsighted or unfair the law, criminals must be punished. As long as Republicans continue to paint themselves into a rhetorical corner, progress on this issue will be at a standstill.

One of the miracles of the times we live in is the ending of discrimination against gays. Unfortunately, it has taken longer than it should have due to the resistance of Republicans, beholden as they are to the religious right for votes. The irony is the GOP has finally begun to understand that gay rights is actually a bedrock conservative issue, which promotes due process, strengthens the institution of marriage, and in particular helps create an opportunity for children to be raised in a legally sanctioned union. The tragedy is that as a society, we could have gotten to the same place years earlier but for conservative intransigence.

I hope that conservative paranoia over immigration reform is the next barrier that will fall. But it will likely be a struggle. For example, Rep. Steve King of Iowa, in an interview on July 18, 2013, with *Newsmax*, said of the Dream Act, which would allow the children of illegal immigrants to obtain citizenship provided they perform well in school and obey the law, that *"for everyone who's a valedictorian, there's another 100 . . . they've got calves the size of cantaloupes because they're hauling 75 pounds of marijuana across the desert."*[13]

Ah yes, those darn calves the size of cantaloupes. Until the Republicans can get rid of this type of sentiment, they will remain a political party tragically handicapped by the attitudes of their past.

Chapter 29: Social Darwinism Is Bogus

Evolution was first explained by Darwin when *On The Origin of Species* was published in 1859. Over the ensuing 150-plus years, scientific understanding of evolution has continuously deepened. In particular, the discovery of DNA, the code by which characteristics are transmitted from one generation to the next, required nearly another century until Watson and Crick published their finding of the double helix in 1953.

Darwin introduced the concept of "survival of the fittest," a term which has been widely misunderstood and misapplied outside of biology. What Darwin and modern biologists mean by this is reproductive fitness, the ability to successfully mate and produce offspring who will do the same.

Consider a simple example, the interplay between a predator and its prey. On the African savannah, a zebra that can run just a little bit faster than average will be more likely to avoid lions and therefore will stand better odds than the rest of the herd at not being eaten. This is what Darwin meant by fitness. Similarly, a lion that can run a little bit faster than average will have a better shot at a zebra dinner.

Examples like this abound. Consider continental drift. As the original landmass of Pangaea broke up into recognizable continents, feeding and nesting grounds for certain birds gradually drifted apart, a process that has continued for millions of years. Today, the great migrators such as the sooty shearwater, which flies over 40,000 miles annually from New Zealand to the North Pacific, represent the power of natural selection to effect great change, given enough time. The sooty shearwater's migratory route probably drifted by a few inches a year, and in each generation, the ability to fly just a little bit longer was "selected" for, resulting in the champion long-distance aviator it has evolved into today.

What survival of the fittest is definitely *not* about is any kind of value judgment that determines one species is "fitter" than any other in the sense of being better or preferred by nature. Biologists would not compare a zebra to a lion and say one is a more desirable species.

Social Darwinism, a term that has been used to promote eugenics and to argue against benevolent social policies, is a pseudoscience that borrows from the vocabulary of genuine Darwinism. However, social Darwinism has it exactly backward. Trying to prevent "undesirables" from breeding means that one doesn't want to live in a world governed by natural selection, since the very fact that—pick your favorite ethnic group to hate—Jews, Blacks, Italians, Irish, Mexicans, etc. have to be reined in means that by Darwinian standards, they have demonstrated their "fitness."

Another discredited concept of social Darwinism is the argument that modern technology and a social safety net are "unnatural." Nature is unmistakably cruel, "red in tooth and claw" as Tennyson said, and therefore a society which is harsh and cruel comes closer to what nature "wants."

But this view is just simply wrong. Nature takes many forms and includes species that are highly social and cooperative. Consider again the example of zebras. One knows from nature documentaries that they live in herds. Since natural selection is a useful backward-looking device, this fact tells us that life in herds provides benefits. If that were not the case, then zebras would have solitary living arrangements, like orangutans, as that would have conferred an evolutionary advantage. Examples can be found in nature that represent just about any social viewpoint one would like to advocate, from species that nurture their young to those who eat them.

People who are racist or just plain mean and are indifferent to the suffering of others don't have Darwin on their side, any more than the Nazis did with their veneer of phony racial science lacquered over a policy of anti-Semitism. If you think people should be allowed to starve on the street, you have overlooked that humanity evolved in groups, with a greater amount of social interdependence than any other life-form on earth. Social Darwinism is just a relatively recent label for selfishness, on the order of "Let them eat cake." Disregard it.

Chapter 30: The Meaning of Life

What is the purpose of existence? Is the fundamental reason for being alive to compose a moving piano sonata, paint a beautiful picture that will hang in a museum and bring pleasure to millions of people over centuries, or make a brilliant scientific discovery that will save lives and improve the human condition? Well, those all seem to be noble objectives, but unfortunately they are not central to life's mission. The real purpose of life is procreation. Lest you think there is a whiff of homophobia in that remark, note that I have a gay son and a PFLAG sticker on my car; I'll place my pro-LBGT rights bona fides up against anyone's.

Consider the premise of this question, which is the attempt to justify why we are here in the first place. A truly satisfying answer requires someone who is either much smarter than me or more confident in their religious beliefs. (I'll avoid the cheap pun that those qualities might stand diametrically opposed to each other.) I'll sidestep the fundamental problem—the purpose of life—and focus on the fact of existence as a starting point. Notice that the mere fact of our existence shows we are the descendants of organisms who managed to successfully reproduce. We are around today because they were able to do two things well: produce offspring and sustain those offspring until they were able to survive to sexual maturity and produce offspring themselves.

One of the constant tensions of human life is the struggle between our animal natures and our spiritual goals. We long to be moral, ethical, just, and fair, but we also want to sometimes get naked and grunt from the pleasures of physical intimacy. Religious leaders from Moses to today have consistently denounced our lustfulness and immorality. In modern times, "culture" is often blamed, as if culture is some abstract attribute of the world that we just happen to be subject to, like floods, tornadoes, and earthquakes. But culture isn't something that merely exists; it's created by and reflects the totality of humanity's tastes and desires. To blame elements of our culture like TV, movies, or pop music for inflaming people's base sexual instincts is a circular argument. Culture is a human creation, which means that to blame it for focusing on sex is just another way to say that people think about, write about, make movies about, and sing about sex because people are fascinated and interested in sex. When we aren't busily engaged in it, we like to talk about it. (The older you get the talking more and more replaces the doing.)

Certainly, we had ancestors who preferred to take long walks in the forest together instead of to hump like, well, animals. Those ancestors, however, didn't produce offspring. The ones who did were near the campfire, plying their potential romantic conquests with caveman moonshine, talking the music of love, and hoping to get lucky.

The scientist Richard Dawkins, in his book *The Selfish Gene*, argues that living organisms are just DNA's way to reproduce, hence the book's title. Humans, and all other life forms, are just convenient mechanisms that genes have developed to perpetuate themselves. Whether this is true or not is sort of beside the point, since Dawkins acknowledges that he describes processes that occur without any actual consciousness.[14] Genes literally cannot be selfish—they just act as if they are.

But this argument is powerful because it helps us understand so much about what drives human behavior. Sex is intensely pleasurable and the urge to find sexual fulfillment can almost feel like a trance. The reason sex is so much fun is because it's central to producing descendants (at least, until cloning gets perfected).

This seems to be an argument that the purpose of life is to have sex, which leads to reproduction. I'm trying to figure out what the counterpoint is, but I am at a loss. Maybe it is to compose a piano sonata. But I can't seem to convince myself.

Chapter 31: Show Me the Money

Once we understand the centrality of sex, so much of the rest of our lives make sense. In middle school, our janitor was a young man who I will refer to as Alan. One day after basketball practice, a few of my friends and I chatted with him in the hallway. Alan told us that the single most important thing in life was money because, in his memorable words, "If you have money, you can always get pussy."

As you might imagine, this wisdom, received at the tender age of 12, left a very deep and lasting impression on me. And lest you think that Alan, as he pushed his janitor's cart with his mop and cleaning supplies, was crude or uncouth, consider the ancient Jewish version, *Ain kemach, ain Torah:* If there is no flour, there is no Torah. The broader explanation is that without resources, there can be no learning or spiritual growth.

No flour, no Torah. Enough money, enough . . . ahem, relations with women. Seems to make sense.

Chapter 32: You Can Be Articulate and Wrong

A classic book about biology is *The Lives of a Cell: Notes of a Biology Watcher*, a collection of 29 essays by physician and researcher Lewis Thomas, first published in 1974. This book is a deeply passionate and beautifully moving work that deals with the interconnectedness of life. It is nothing less than a minor masterpiece, fully deserving of its widespread praise and popularity.

Thomas focused primarily on living organisms but also drew some inferences about the possible future impact of computers on human development. When it came to biology, Thomas was in his element, yet on the subject of computers, he was way off the mark. In a passage about the potential of artificial intelligence to someday replicate the complexity of human thought, Thomas wrote that for this to happen, there would need to be "three billion" computers, about the world's population at the time, and a number which one presumes he chose to convey a sense of the preposterous. Thomas observed that he doubted anyone could fund such a project, "much less make room." Plus, these computers would have to be "wired together" and "communicating with each other . . . incessantly." With all of these improbabilities layered on top of one another, he concluded, this state of affairs won't occur for a "long time ahead."[15]

Billions of computers networked together and in constant communication? Hmm, sounds like Thomas predicted the Internet, except that in his view such an endeavor would be too big and expensive to occur any time in the foreseeable future. Despite his genius as a biologist, he simply couldn't envision that computing devices the size of filing cabinets would someday be shrunk to the dimensions of a deck of cards and that the cost of computing power would shrink even more. There are probably more than "three billion of them" already since researcher IDC reports that sales of "smart connected devices" (smart phones, tablets, and personal computers) were 1.2 billion units in 2012 alone, and they are indeed all wired together.[16]

Thomas's argument against artificial intelligence

rested primarily on the assumption that billions of interconnected computers were simply unimaginable for reasons of cost and logistics. But he expressed himself with grace and elegance, in a prose style that is seductively persuasive. I would be content with just a pinkie's worth of his brains and literary skills. But still, note that when he strayed from his area of expertise—biology—to one where he was simply another amateur—computer technology—he was as wrong as the rest of us. Keep that in mind the next time a prediction about the future seems utterly convincing.

Chapter 33: Adults Can Be Stupid

To small children, adults are almost godlike in comparison. Compared to a toddler, a 6-foot tall, 200-pound man is a towering giant. And the knowledge and wisdom of adults is also of a profoundly different quality than that of children. Our vocabulary is larger. We can comprehend more sophisticated concepts, like the plot of a romantic comedy with Jennifer Aniston. We know how to use utensils while we eat, how to wipe our behinds after use of the restroom, and how to text while behind the wheel of a car. Small children, on the other hand, possess none of these amazing faculties, and the gulf between a 3-year-old and a 30-year-old is enormous. Well, they probably can text better than us, but their feet can't reach the gas pedal yet.

Gradually, however, kids learn that not all adults are smart. In fact, since the distribution of intelligence, like many other characteristics, forms a bell-shaped curve, about half of kids will be smarter than half the adults that surround them by the time they grow up. And middle school is when they start to realize it. Kids begin to understand that a lot of the concepts that have been stuffed into them are wrong, or at least not something they personally agree with. Children of conservatives become liberals. Children of religious believers become atheists. Children of potheads become alcohol drinkers.

How dumb are we adults? Consider that we are responsible for baseball, a sport in which grown men tug at their crotches and spit when television cameras turn in their direction. We believe in all kinds of wacky conspiracy theories: the government hid the existence of aliens from us; JFK's assassination was an inside job; 9/11 was an inside job; fluoride in drinking water is a Communist plot (I still haven't been able to figure out why an improvement in the dental health of America helps our enemies); all kinds of strange ideas about Masons, Catholics, and Jews; and the wonders of the ancient world, like the great pyramids of Egypt, were built by aliens. (What is it with aliens, anyway? Why can't they help us with modern projects like the development of better wireless networks? How come the ancient Mayans had all the luck?) Meanwhile, from behind their iPads, the kids definitely notice that an awful lot of adults are complete goofballs. Once children start to comprehend that they are smarter than many of the older folks around them who are in charge, life starts to develop a *Rise of the Planet of the Apes* quality to it, with a rebellion inevitably in the offing. Which reminds me, I've got to make sure I lock the kids' cages before I go to sleep tonight.

Chapter 34: You Have Two Brains

You've heard of the term "gut decision." The meaning is literal: a decision based on what you feel in your stomach. It turns out that people actually have two systems for processing information, with both effectively being brains. The one that most people mean when they refer to the word is a wrinkled mound of gelatinous tissue inside their skulls. But there also is a parallel one that contains your digestive tract.

In the middle school years, these two decision-making systems are in competition with one another. Teachers want you to focus on the brain inside your head, drilling you on fractions and the basics of the five-paragraph essay. But you are distracted by the other brain, located below the esophagus, the one that causes you to fall in love, that is attuned to the music of the universe. This is the internal force that makes you impulsive, that moves you to dance, to burst with joy for no particular reason, the brain that teachers hate and adults want to squash.

When we are younger, most of us have some sort

of expectation about how our romantic life will unfold. Usually, there is some type of analytical aspect to this. If you like to play Scrabble, you'll be attracted to a potential mate who also enjoys tiled word games. If you have an affinity for hiking, you'll be drawn to people who love the outdoors. If your favorite sport is tennis, you expect to date others who play it for recreation as well.

But then something unexpected happens. You stand in a crowded room and suddenly notice you have eyes for only one person. You know nothing about them except that you just heard the faint sound of harps in the background. Then, joy of joys, you learn the other person feels the same way. As you get to know each other, you discover that she finds Scrabble tedious, tennis boring, and considers any type of lodging at the level of a Motel 6 to be the equivalent of camping. And yet you fall in love anyway, completely helpless. The brain in your head tries to tell you to slow down. But your stomach says, "Wow, what a smile. What sparkling eyes. I've simply got to get to know that girl better." At this point, the rational processes you once relied on are irrelevant.

I have some simple advice in this regard: trust your gut. It's always right.

Chapter 35: As a Kid, You Lack Perspective

When I was 14 years old, I spent a week one summer with my cousins. The family had 3 boys, ages 14, 11, and 9 at the time. During my visit, a stomach bug passed through the house, and all of us became extremely ill, with symptoms that manifested themselves from both ends of the digestive tract. I was struck rather suddenly, after a movie, when we stopped to get ice cream cones. As we stood in the parking lot, I suddenly and without warning erupted in projectile vomiting, spewing out upchuck onto the pavement directly in front of the dad. He quickly pulled my legs back to minimize collateral damage to my shoes and pants.

On the drive home, I told him I thought that the ice cream cone acted as an enzyme that caused me to become suddenly sick. After I said that, the word "enzyme" stuck in my head. A few months earlier during the spring term of seventh grade, we had completed a vocabulary unit in science class and learned the definitions of various terms such as mixture, compound, enzyme, and catalyst. The meanings were still somewhat fresh in my mind. I had intended to say that the ice cream cone was a catalyst, which is something that speeds up a reaction or process. The dessert apparently sped up my nausea, hence the disgusting spectacle I had made of myself. However, to call it an "enzyme" meant effectively nothing in scientific terms. As we drove, I was embarrassed not by the grotesque scene in the parking lot but by the fact I confused my science vocabulary. I was preoccupied with the fear that the dad thought I was not very bright to have mixed up enzyme with catalyst. Note that I did not give a moment's consideration to the offensive display my upset stomach caused.

Such is the lack of perspective of middle schoolers. Keep that in mind when you approach them. Middle schoolers may seem like normal, functional human beings. However, they are anything but. I was there once. I know of what I speak.

Chapter 36: Looking Good Is More Than Skin Deep

One of the greatest complaints by adults about kids is that they are focused on superficial aspects of life, perhaps nowhere more so than the habit of judgments based on appearance. They confuse surface beauty with inner goodness. But we modern humans possess minds that were designed for survival on the African savannah. Combine that with the centrality of sex to the human condition, and the need to not only produce offspring, but to make sure those offspring survive long enough to produce offspring of their own. Lather, rinse, repeat.

Given that human children are dependent on adults for such an absurdly long period of time as compared to other species, those children need adults who are going to be available for many years to take care of them. From an evolutionary standpoint, both health and youth are important because the younger and healthier you are, the more likely that you will be around in the future to help provide for any kids you might have. Which means that youthfulness is a desirable quality in a potential mate since by definition the older you are, the closer you are to your final breath. Hence the joke, live each day as if it will be your last and someday you will be right.

As a result, in every society, at all times, youthfulness is regarded as an attractive characteristic. We may complain that movies and music videos are populated by excessively young and good-looking performers, but let's face it, while it's remarkable the Rolling Stones still tour, do you really want to see elderly musicians with their shirts off in music videos?

I didn't think so.

What else makes people attractive? Humans, along with many other forms of animal life, have what is known as bilateral symmetry, which means that our left and right sides look alike. In fact, this is an approximation. No one has left and right sides that are completely identical, although to the naked eye they may seem that way.

According to *National Geographic,* the difference in bilateral symmetry for most people is around 1–3 percent.[17] They reported on several experiments in which subjects rated people based on attractiveness, and in general, the greater the amount of bilateral symmetry, the higher the rating. *National Geographic* reported that features considered sexy in women, such as wide hips, larger breasts, and long hair, are positively correlated with symmetry. Accordingly, beauty is a fairly reliable "advertisement" for good health. And in prehistoric times, the selection of a healthy mate could mean the difference between life and death for your offspring.

Considering once again the power of natural selection, it makes sense that beauty is valued, even though it may seem superficial. So, when we hit the middle school years and enter puberty, we turn into sexual (or sex-crazed) persons, and the 90–95 percent of us who aren't gay focus like never before on the opposite gender. But while we live in the Internet age, our bodies are still trapped in an evolutionary past. Looks matter . . . a lot. And regardless of what the adults in charge tell us, when your heart starts to flip-flop and your groin begins to rumble, all of the advances in the speed and power of microprocessors are irrelevant.

When I lived on a kibbutz in Israel, I met the woman who made *my* heart flip-flop. I learned the Israeli version of a popular Russian Yiddish folk song, "Tumbalalaika," which dates from the pioneering days during the pre-state "Yishuv" era. Hundreds of thousands of Jews fled persecution in Europe and sought to establish a modern Jewish nation in our ancient homeland.

The Hebrew stanza added to this Yiddish song goes as follows:

> *Mah oseh, oseh hechalutz?*
> *K'sheh who ba, who ba lakibbutz*
> *Who ba lakibbutz, rotze la'avod*
> *Roeh bachura, v'shocheach hakol*

> What is the young pioneer doing?
> When he came to the kibbutz, he wanted to work
> But then he saw a girl, and forgot everything.

Even young, pioneering Jews, consumed with a fervor to reconnect with the land of their ancestors and to live free of persecution, forgot everything when they saw a pretty girl (as I did as well). Asking teenagers to concentrate on the fine details of the Stamp Act of 1765, while a sea of hormones churns through their endocrine system, is like an attempt to hold back the tides.

Chapter 37: I Didn't Go to the Worst High School

I contend that the institution of high school in America is terrible, both educationally and socially. For the longest time, I assumed that I went to the worst high school in the world, the eponymously named South Brunswick High School, located in South Brunswick, New Jersey, which I attended from 1971–75. How bad was it? Consider the message that our graduating class advisors wrote in the school yearbook:

> We have mixed feelings about having been advisors for the Class of '75. The Class was unfortunately apathetic about many of the activities we attempted . . . as such, it's been a . . . frustrating experience trying to advise this class. The quality of those who have worked to help . . . will, we hope, be recalled more easily than the lack of involvement by their classmates.
>
> We wish the best for . . . the Class of '75. It

*is not an altogether promising world you
would encounter.*

This is from the two teachers handpicked to work
with our class as our official advisors! In case their
meaning is not obvious, let me translate in more
direct terms:

*Wow, were you guys a disappointment.
Even by the low standards of your
generation, the Class of '75 still managed
to surprise us by your torpor and lack of
intellectual curiosity. However, the adult
world is no picnic, and now you get to be
a part of it. Sayonara!*

Probably any high school in America in the 1970s
would have been awful, but for pure misery, it's
tough to top New Jersey. Parts of the Garden State
are absolutely beautiful: the Pinelands, the Delaware
Water Gap, and miles of coastline. Unfortunately,
that's not where South Brunswick is located. It lies
midway between New York and Philadelphia, and
when I grew up, it consisted mostly of suburban

sprawl surrounded by rural poverty. I'm told that today the community is a lot nicer. Well, that's no big deal; lots of places are nicer today. You couldn't even visit many areas of New York City in broad daylight in the 1970s for fear of violent crime. When I started business school in 1983, New York was in the very early stages of recovery from its nadir. A couple of enterprising Columbia students found a rolled up rug set out on the curb for garbage pickup. They brought the rug back up to their dorm room, and when they unrolled it, they found a corpse inside.

One of the reasons my secondary education seemed so disappointing was because I went to high school at a time when the country seethed with racial tension. How bad was it? Consider the following story. A friend of mine in Seattle was from the suburban area immediately outside of Newark, NJ, which also happens to be Philip Roth territory. My friend told me that one of his childhood memories was being awakened by his father in the middle of the night when he was around eight or nine years old. The family was about to jump into the car in order to take a surprise vacation.

His dad said, "Don't bother to pack or change out of your pajamas, and oh, by the way, take your baseball bat with you."

He recalls they drove through the night to Atlantic City, where they checked into a hotel and then shopped for underwear and clothing. Many years later, he asked his dad, "Do you remember that vacation to Atlantic City we started out on in the middle of the night?"

His father said, "That was no vacation. We ran from the Newark riots."

This was an outburst of violence that lasted five days in July 1967, which resulted in 26 deaths, over 700 injuries, and extensive property damage.[18] While Newark was the most extreme example, other communities were impacted as well. Smaller towns, such as nearby New Brunswick, the next town over from where I grew up, also had a minor riot of its own, as did many other communities throughout the region.

We were not immune to the racial tension of this era in our suburban enclave. When I went to high school, the student body was about 90 percent white and 10 percent black, but it seemed like most of the black students felt a (justifiable) sense of grievance. In my sophomore year, a female black student claimed that a teacher told her to take off her "n-word" hat. The teacher denied this, but for the next week, she was personally escorted by a uniformed police officer from class to class.

We had a gym teacher, Mr. Petko, who had been a member of the 1956 Hungarian Olympic wrestling team before defecting from Communism and fleeing to America. He looked like he had been carved out of a block of granite. Mr. Petko often remarked that the school should just throw all the white kids and all the black kids into the gym, lock the doors, pit them against one another in a death match, and whoever came out alive would be in charge.

Even though our community was middle class, the high school was in a constant state of disrepair from a combination of neglect and vandalism. On rainy days, a barrel was put out in the main hallway to catch drops from a leaky roof. The stalls in the boys' bathrooms had their doors ripped off. The restrooms were so filthy and disgusting that using them was out of the question anyway. There was a phone booth outside the school that was typically rendered inoperable from assault by the students.

Curiously, the toilets in the boys' locker room were not vandalized, probably because even the toughest of the school's bullies could have been torn to shreds in an instant by Mr. Petko. However, in my freshman year, I noticed that in the boys' locker room stalls, once the toilet paper ran out, it was never restocked. And it was old, industrial-style paper, the type that is pulled down from a slot, one folded sheet at a time, like an upside-down tissue box. Unless the janitor had replicated his work environment at home, it would have been pointless for him to have stolen it for personal use. I suspect he probably didn't bother to check the paper supply when he made his evening rounds and figured that given the general malaise, no one would ever complain. Accordingly, the first day of school of my sophomore, junior, and senior years, during gym class, I made it a point to open the metal toilet paper holder and take out a substantial stack to store in my locker as my own personal stash for the balance of the year.

A good example of the poor educational quality of our school is represented by my experience in Spanish class. Our teacher, Dr. Martinez, was a lovely woman. On a personal level, I thoroughly enjoyed her company. She had been the wife of the Dominican Republic's ambassador to the United States. She represented the upper crust of Dominican society, and with the title "Doctor" in front of her name, she clearly was a highly educated woman. However, after her husband had passed away, it appeared the pension granted to the wife of a deceased Dominican Republic diplomat was not sufficient to live on, so she became a Spanish teacher late in life. She approached the job with a large degree of independence, and we would typically spend our class time listening to her recount stories from her marriage and the glamorous social life that her late husband's career allowed for.   Once in a while, she would make a half-hearted attempt to actually teach something. On those rare occasions, she would usually inform us that we were going to practice the "*gerundio.*" She might as well have told us we were going to attempt to read ancient Egyptian hieroglyphics. I had absolutely no idea what a *gerundio* was, and whatever we practiced sailed completely over the top of my head.

Many years later, by random coincidence, I happened to stumble across the word "gerund" in English. A gerund is the form that a verb takes when it ends in "ing." "Walking" is therefore the gerund form of the verb "to walk." I connected the dots . . . gerund . . . *gerundio*. So that's what she was talking about!

But here's the thing. I thought my high school was the worst in the country while I attended it. But then through random coincidence, I happened to join the board of an education technology company as part of my career in high tech. I spent about 10 years in the business side of education, including co-founding an online high school that was eventually sold to the parent company of the University of Phoenix. Through this process, I became more knowledgeable than I would have ever wanted to be about the problems of the American education system. If I thought things were bad where I went to school, it was only because I had no idea how much worse they were elsewhere. According to The Alliance for Education Excellence, only about 78 percent of American high school students earn their regular diplomas (although a significant number of dropouts eventually receive the less challenging GED).[19] My high school was actually better than average.

And let me add a coda to this story. The community I grew up in, South Brunswick, has seen a significant surge in population, with much of the influx from skilled professionals. In particular, the region has seen a large amount of growth in its Indian community. (I am tempted to say that anyone who thinks immigration is a bad thing is an idiot, but that would be unkind, so let me just say they are misinformed.)

The shithole of a building I spent four miserable years in has been replaced by a gleaming, expensive new structure about three times the size. Presumably, the bathroom stalls now have both doors *and* paper. The township itself has been recognized as one of the top places in the country to live by the sort of magazines that compile those types of lists. Should any current residents of South Brunswick read this, I suspect my description of the prior era might be similar to reading about the sordid past of many of the gentrified neighborhoods in New York such as Brooklyn or the far West Side of Manhattan, which were once rundown and derelict, but today are prime locations for hipsters.

So I didn't go to the worst high school in America. It just felt like it.

Chapter 38: Profits Come Before Feelings

A lot of jobs crush the human spirit, and if that isn't bad enough, there is the additional risk of having a difficult boss. The tragedy is that managers and supervisors don't even want to be bad people. But they have to follow orders from *their* bosses to hang onto their jobs, and the problem is that in any well-run company, the goal is not the happiness of employees but making money. Anytime those objectives come into conflict, guess which one wins.

Actually, there is one type of work environment where the happiness of the employees does matter and that is where the workers are represented by a union. But except for monopolies like government where tax dollars keep enterprises running regardless of how awful the performance, unionized companies typically fail against non-union competition. According to the US Bureau of Labor Statistics, union members accounted for over 30 percent of all private sector employees 50 years ago.[20] That number has been shrinking steadily and today is in the single digits.

 Ed Harris

If you want to understand why, here's a simple explanation. Do you think Google would be more successful if its employees joined a labor union? In the battle of profits vs. happiness, profits win every time. But that may not be as bad as it seems. The next chapter explains this seeming contradiction.

Chapter 39: Capitalism Is Good

Big companies are evil, right? That's been the accepted wisdom forever and is practically treated as religious dogma on most college campuses. Students may express their contempt of "the man" before they finish their studies. But they nonetheless dream of landing a good job with a profitable company in order to pay off their student loans once they graduate. It's easy in the abstract to think that when it comes to business, big equals bad. But what about: Whole Foods, which represents a quantum leap in terms of supermarket quality; Starbucks, who has led a revolution in coffee standards; Apple, innovator of so many great technologies; Google, same as Apple; Tesla, which is building electric cars; Target, which has made discount retailing chic; Urban Outfitters, which offers great style at moderate prices; H&M, same as Urban Outfitters; and Amazon, which has almost single-handedly made e-commerce possible?

Another thing about big companies—they have often led the way on civil rights. In their case, the motivation is financial—they want to avoid lawsuits.

Their policies may be designed to protect their financial health, but the outcome is still good for everyone. For many years, most big companies have forbidden discrimination on the basis of sexual orientation, even as states and the federal government have often dragged their feet.

I recall a colleague of mine 20 years ago from Texas who considered himself to be a person of religious faith. Once, in a conversation about the trend of business casual clothing, he shared with me that he refused to wear Dockers because at the time they were one of the first big corporations to extend benefits to the partners of gay employees. I don't know if this guy still holds his homophobic views today, but if he does, either his wife makes his trousers for him or he walks around in his undershorts.

Corporations are good for the reason that people hate them—all they care about is profits. It used to be that the key to business success was industrial heft, such as having the biggest factory or the largest coal mine. It was said that the big ate the small. Now it's more often the case that the fast eat the slow.

Today, in the computer age, most businesses need smart employees that are well-educated, adept at using technology, flexible, and are good problem-solvers. You can't attract these types of workers if your official motto is, "We Hate Gay People." Well, you probably could attract a certain former colleague of mine, but he might find the office awfully lonely.

Chapter 40: Adults Resent Kids for a Good Reason

For kids, one of the greatest riddles is why adults are constantly in a crabby mood. When we first moved to Seattle, we had neighbors who we became friendly with. I'll call them Frank and Betty. We had one child at the time, our daughter, who was an infant. Frank and Betty were an older childless couple. Given their ages and attitude, it looked like their intention was to go through life unburdened by expense and chaos of lineal descendants.

Our apartment complex teemed with young families. There was a playground outside our building, and it was constantly filled with the joyful sound of children, music to my wife's ears as a full-time, stay-at-home mom. Frank and Betty, on the other hand, always complained about the racket. To them it was unnecessary and annoying "screaming."

When I was in the second grade, it began snowing one day during class. As a little kid, snow was one of the most exciting things that existed. All the children ran to the window to look out in elation. The teacher, a particularly sour woman, reprimanded us in a sarcastic tone, saying "What's the matter, haven't you ever seen snow before?"

My wife, I have to say, is an exception to the general adult rule. She has always viewed laughter and play as the most important priority. When our kids were small, their days were filled with a whirlwind of activities. But many adults seem to resent how much fun kids have, how much noise they make, and the general mess that they create.

And then as one gets older, no matter how energetic, healthy, or beautiful you once were, you will decline with age. It doesn't have to be as awful as it sounds. Most people who maintain healthy lifestyles will be fit and active for a very long time. And at least for us guys, with all the erectile dysfunction drugs on the market, one of the worst things for men about the aging process now can be solved with a simple pill. (Just for the record, I work out regularly and have enough cardiovascular health to not have to worry about *that* issue.)

The reason most adults complain about the sounds of laughter coming from the playground is simple. We're jealous!

Chapter 41: It's Not Too Hard to Fake It

Life generally offers two options to get ahead—work really hard at being successful or fake it along the way. But deception can only succeed if it appears authentic. I recall a vacation I took with my parents when I was 16 years old. We went to the Fontainebleau Hotel in Miami Beach, at the time the top location in town (and featured in the 1964 James Bond movie *Goldfinger*). In those days, at big resort hotels, parents went off and did adult stuff, and teenagers were left to entertain themselves.

One evening I found myself in the lobby with another high schooler about the same age, both of us with no plans. We talked about what you would have expected a pair of male adolescents to talk about: girls. My new acquaintance was exceptionally boastful about his ability to pick up young ladies. He was a master at it, he said, and he described at great length his unparalleled skill to engage the interest and attention of the opposite sex. About five minutes into his description of his wondrous powers as a pickup artist, we spied two teenage girls headed in our direction across the lobby. Mr. Smooth Operator suddenly lowered his voice, and in an urgent whisper said, "Why don't you go ahead and pick them up for us. I'm a bit out of practice."

He was, as they say in Texas, all hat and no saddle. Clearly he did not possess the ability to pick up girls. But his lack of skill would not have mattered if he could just fake an air of confidence. Because when you get right down to it, there really is no difference in most endeavors between genuine quality and the counterfeit version. Obviously, in some fields, like medicine, qualifications matter. But when it comes to corporate management, joke telling, or to pretending that you are smart, just about anyone can do it.

In business, I've at times worked for and alongside people who made terrible decisions. (I imagine the same has been thought about me on many an occasion.) Very smart folks can still make not-so-smart choices.

For example, in the early 1990s I joined the management team of a company that put phones on commercial airplanes. It seemed like a good idea at the time. This was at a time when growth in the cell phone business was beginning to accelerate like mad. Our company was an affiliate of one of the leading wireless operators. They were signing up new subscribers so fast they could barely keep up with demand.

Our division spent a fortune on technology and equipment. There was just one problem—passengers didn't seem to have much interest in the service.

Part of the problem was the design. The phones were recessed into the seatbacks, attached by a cord, and required the swipe of a credit card. And since the ambient noise level inside an airplane is quite high, it's hard to talk over the din. Finally in coach where most people are seated, passengers are jammed in elbow-to-elbow, and it's impossible to have any privacy.

In order for the service to be of any value, we had to put a network of ground cell stations across the entire country, since planes fly everywhere, even places where not a lot of people are to be found. Add it all up, and our losses, relative to the size of our small business, were substantial.

But then AT&T came along and bought our corporate parent for so many billions that if you started to count on your fingers, you'd eventually have to take off your shoes and socks and use your toes. We went along for the ride at a premium valuation. My colleagues and I regarded the entire endeavor as a success, especially once we got our hands on our share of the pie, and most of my peers went on to high-powered jobs elsewhere. Under AT&T's ownership, the service groaned along, until they finally shut it down completely after many years of continued losses.

But who cares? We looked like we were successful and that's all that mattered. I suggest you try it yourself.

Chapter 42: Pretend to Be Smart

Being smart, like being successful, is hard and may not always be worth the effort. I have a suggestion that reduces the workload. Rather than spending a large chunk of your life studying, consider the lazy way to be smart—use foreign phrases and buzzwords. Why say "end of the century" when you can use the French version, *fin de siècle*?

Anyone can be bored, but only a true sophisticate can have ennui. In business, rather than talk about what product or service you sell, refer to the "vertical" you are in, or even better, the "space." Instead of running a hot dog stand, you can be in the "portable food and dining space."

In college, when I found myself a few credits short of graduation in my senior year, I took a summer film studies class. The professor talked about how movies had been transformed from entertainment to an academic and intellectual pursuit, along with the type of snobbery such a transformation often entails. I went to college before Barnes & Noble grew into a big national chain. Back then, their entire operation consisted of two cavernous stores in lower Manhattan, facing each other on the same block, one that sold regular books, both new and used, and the other that carried used textbooks. In the New York area, it was usually a good idea to see if you could find your textbooks at Barnes & Noble before heading over to the campus bookstore.

I went there after I enrolled in the film class and asked a store clerk if they had a section for movies. He gave me a withering stare, as if I had asked where they stashed the pornography, and replied, with icy contempt, "We do not carry books about movies."

I then rephrased the question, asking if they had a section devoted to texts about film studies.

"Oh, yes, you can find them in aisle four."

Learn to talk fancy instead of plain. If you see a once great thing decline, don't say "what a shame" but rather *sic transit gloria mundi*, "there goes the glory of the world."

It's an easy trick, once you get used to it. After all, *après moi, le deluge*.

Chapter 43: Small Country Syndrome

My Canadian friend Jules suffers what I like to refer to as Small Country Syndrome. This malady consists of the belief that Americans are, underneath our prosperity and military strength, a nation of uncultured ignoramuses. Yes, I know that Canada is geographically vast, larger in fact than the United States. But its population is only one-tenth of ours, and much of it is empty wasteland. It qualifies as a small country, its millions of square miles (oops, sorry, kilometers) of frozen tundra notwithstanding.

In one of our conversations, Jules used the word "ellipsis," and then added, "Ed, that's what you call it when you see 'dot, dot, dot' in a quote, meaning that some text has been skipped."

He assumed, given his affliction with Small Country Syndrome, it would be unlikely that an American, even one with a college degree, would have command of a tenth grade vocabulary. I spat a stream of tobacco juice with disdain into a tin can that I carry around for just such a purpose. Then I hitched up my bib overalls and informed him that I did in fact know what an ellipsis was. I had once come across the word by accident while searching online for tickets to a monster truck rally. A moment of discord in a longstanding friendship passed, and we hugged, with Jules contrite enough to even quickly check my pelt for fleas during our embrace.

Since I have lived in Holland and am married to a Dutch girl, I am very familiar with Small Country Syndrome because so many citizens of the Netherlands suffer from it. Take any country with a population under 50 million fortunate enough to possess a democratic form of government, a strong education system, and a high standard of living, and it seems inevitable for the locals to assume that their society is superior to the United States. It's the international equivalent of the blonde joke. If the good-looking girl is smart, too, then the universe would be cruel and heartless. In order to maintain faith in a just and benevolent Creator, we assume that an advantage in one attribute must be offset by a deficit in another.

And it's not just that America is the world's sole remaining superpower, it's that we are so blithely unconcerned about any threats to our dominance. While Angela Merkel, the Chancellor of Germany, and Nicolas Sarkozy, the President of France, are busy declaring that multiculturalism is a failed experiment, we're on our way to the supermarket to get fresh hummus and figure out if Hanukkah falls over Christmas break. Oh, and don't forget to pick up the Quinceañera present for the neighbor's daughter on the way home.

Americans brim with an overconfidence that borders on arrogance. Let Al Gore grow a beard and rail against our materialistic way of life. He can collect all the Nobel prizes he likes and travel by private plane, which allows him to generate a carbon footprint nearly as large as his bank account. Bloomberg estimates that Mr. Gore's net worth is in excess of $200 million and reported that in 2007, according to a public records request, his Nashville home used 20 times the national average for electricity consumption.[21] Meanwhile, the rest of us, not quite as stupendously wealthy as the former vice president, are heading over to Costco to buy mayonnaise in quantities sufficient to fill a Jacuzzi, before we settle in at home to watch a new episode of *American Idol*.

A number of years ago, my Dutch niece visited our family with her equally Dutch boyfriend. Like most Europeans, he had traveled internationally, but only to a variety of little countries of the type that you could fit into Idaho with room left over. After about a week, he came up to my wife, overcome with emotion. He had never personally been to the United States before, and he was certain he would find upon his arrival a racist, violent society. He wanted to apologize for his (unbeknownst to us) negative perception of America, not that he had been anything but a polite houseguest. But he marveled at the sheer ordinariness of a Jewish family with white parents and (two out of three) brown kids, living with Chinese, Russian, Korean, Mexican, and Indian neighbors, everyone in a whirlwind of motion in their minivans to get to soccer practice or piano lessons. He expected an America of street gangs, burned-out buildings and graffiti, not the land of smoothie bars and Starbucks, of yoga pants and jogging strollers. Misconceptions sometimes die hard. And sometimes blondes are brilliant.

That sound you just heard is God laughing.

Chapter 44: Logic Makes No Sense

There is a well-known logic exercise called the Wason Selection Test, named after the person who developed it in 1966, psychologist Peter Cathcart Wason.[22] In the original version, subjects are shown four playing cards, two showing the letters "A" and "D" and two showing the numbers "4" and "7". Subjects are then asked which cards they should turn over to test the following rule: If a card has a vowel on one side, then it has an even number on the other side.

Sounds kind of tricky, but solvable, one would think. However, in Wason's initial experiments, only four percent of the participants were able to come up with the correct answer. The most common mistake was to turn over the card showing "4". But the rule is that cards with vowels have an even number on the opposite side. It is silent about whether even-numbered cards are required to have a vowel.

The correct answer is to turn over the card with "A" because if it has an odd number on the other side the rule is violated, and turn over the "7" because if it has a vowel on the other side that would also violate the rule.

This problem turned out to be devilishly difficult to solve and is even rather complex to explain concisely. But what is even more fascinating is the discovery that if the logic test transformed into a real-life example and not a total abstraction, it becomes dramatically easier to solve.

In a fascinating subsequent experiment in 1982, researchers Griggs and Cox kept the basic structure of the question intact but changed the details.[23] You are in a bar with four people. There are two people whose age you know—19 and 55—but you don't know what they are drinking. There are another two people whose ages you don't know. One has a Coke and the other a beer. If you want to determine if there is any underage drinking going on, who do you check?

Most people get the right answer easily: you check the beverage of the 19-year-old and the ID of the beer drinker. Once the problem is transformed from dry abstract reasoning to something relatable to ordinary human experience, it becomes more intuitive.

What Wason and subsequent researchers discovered is that the ability to think logically is tied to whether a scenario is relatable. People are intuitively good logical thinkers when confronted with problems that reflect human experience. Our brains are designed to navigate the real world, and we are quite good at doing so.

So the next time you hear a teacher complain that students don't understand how to think logically, you will now be armed with the facts to contradict them.

Chapter 45: Figure Out How to Get Rid of the Body

In the fall of 1975, one ordinary day at sunset, a festive group of American and European youth serving as volunteers on Kibbutz Shefayim, 20 minutes north of Tel Aviv on Israel's coastal plain, hiked along a trail and down a steep cliff to the beach for a bonfire and an evening of raucous festivity. We revelers were fortified by Arak, a distilled spirit of the Levant, popular for both its powerful anise flavor and an alcohol content that unsheathes one's scimitar faster than you can say "Ali Baba." The young men and women who comprised the party were in for an evening of songs, laughter, and the potential of romance. I had been in a near-priapic state myself ever since arriving at this lush paradise a few months earlier, surrounded by fragrant citrus fields (the word "paradise" comes from the Hebrew for fruit grove, *pardes*) and an equally captivating scent of ripening young women, whose own fruit-bearing limbs left me quivering like a tuning fork.

As the sun went down and promise of love was in the air, my roommate, Dave Goldberg, appeared to be making considerable progress with a young Scandinavian lass, who had arrived at the kibbutz earlier that week. As Dave was engaged in amorous pursuit, he suddenly discovered that the girl he appeared to be frisking for contraband went from drunk to unconscious. He sheepishly came to the realization that his advances were not being rebuffed because his potential conquest had a mutual attraction but rather due to the fact she had passed out.

As the rest of us became aware of what had happened, and after we disregarded Dave's obvious embarrassment, our first thought was how to get this poor girl back to her dorm room and up a steep hill a good half mile away. It turned out that she was sturdily built, not fat exactly, but with a frame that would have lent itself to playing power forward for Trondheim State's women's basketball team. As the Vietnam War protestors demonstrated, a completely limp adult body is nearly impossible to lift and carry. The slackness made the dead weight feel like it had been doubled. We tried to hoist our Swedish farmer's daughter by the undignified approach of each of four

163

young men, present company included, grabbing an arm or leg, but after just a few strenuous and lurching steps we realized that even this technique would leave us totally exhausted long before we got to our intended destination. Then one of us had a brilliant idea: get an empty wheelbarrow by the farm shed, dump her in, and roll her back home, which is exactly what we did.

The next morning, we found out from her roommate that the young lady in question awoke to find said wheelbarrow outside her door. She left the kibbutz the same day in abject shame. No one even recalled her name, and all we knew was that she was one of the newly arrived crop of nearly identical Nordic blondes—in her case, perhaps a bit more well-knit and ready to join a roller derby team than her compatriots. Dave ended up frustrated in his passion, but as I recall, he took the whole incident with a dollop of wry amusement.

And I learned two valuable lessons. One, if you ever decide that murder is a good idea and your intended victim is larger than a ferret, you'd better have a good plan for how to dispose of the body. And secondly, I was going to have to develop some game if I wanted to get on the playing field myself (something that I appear to have eventually accomplished, as I have successfully procreated). As for Dave, I suspect he learned a greater appreciation for the subtle distinction between a girl donning Arak goggles and losing consciousness.

And, to this day, if I close my eyes and let my memory wander, I can still smell the fragrance of nature's beautiful creations—vegetable and animal alike—ripening in the warm Mediterranean climate, where a paradise on land meets the intoxicating romantic scent of the beach.

Chapter 46: Literal Meanings Are Meaningless

"We hold these truths to be self-evident, that all men are created equal." This phrase from the preamble of the US Constitution is engraved in our collective consciousness as Americans, but what exactly does it mean? The words are powerful only because we know that all men are *not* created equal. The moral force of this concept is unstated but clearly implied: even though men are not alike, they all should be treated so under the law. Some men are rich and some are poor. Some have brilliant intellects and some are dull. Some easily win affection from the ladies, and some need a haircut and new wardrobe. Some are gifted athletically, and some, like me, are doomed to sports mediocrity. But the law doesn't favor the rich over the poor, the strong over the weak, or Michael Jordan over the man with the one-inch vertical leap.

Even while the ink was still drying upon the parchment the Constitution, the debate over its meaning had already commenced. The question of whether the "men" whose equality was self-evident should be limited just to white men, or white men and women, or whites and blacks, has taken our society over 200 years to resolve. Slavery endured for a century and Jim Crow segregation for another 100 years.

We don't know if Thomas Jefferson hoped that someday blacks would be freed from slavery and women could fully participate in every aspect of American life, but today we are the fortunate beneficiaries of an expansive interpretation of a living document. Yes, tradition is at times a wonderful thing. So is progress.

What is true about our history as a nation is also true for the Bible. The Constitution was drafted in more or less modern English by people who left a vast amount of historical documentation and archival material. We are deeply informed about Colonial America and the lives of the men who created our nation. By comparison, the Bible is opaque and challenging to comprehend. The Old Testament, as Christians refer to the Jewish Bible, is written in an ancient form of Hebrew, not the modern version spoken in Israel today. Even those fully fluent in

Ed Harris

present-day Hebrew struggle to decipher ancient texts with obscure references and confusing grammatical constructions. Also, the language is commonly written without vowels. For example, the Hebrew word "r-d" could mean raid, read, reed, rid, ride, rode, rude, etc. Many passages of the Jewish Bible contain alternative vowel combinations that support different potential readings.

The next time someone tells you that they absolutely positively know that their specific interpretation of the Jewish Bible should be regarded as the equivalent of God's own word, remember that every generation has a moral obligation to study the truth and understand what it means in their own times. Jefferson kept the slaves in their chains, Lincoln freed them, and Johnson let their descendants eat at lunch counters. The three of them were inspired by the same concept that all men are created equal. The path to morality cannot take the arc of human progress out of the equation.

Chapter 47: The Sexual Revolution Was Overrated

Every book or documentary about the 1960s talks about the introduction of oral contraceptives (the pill) and the sexual revolution that this medical breakthrough helped usher in. Well, I was there, and let me tell you, it was not as dramatic as you might think. Even though everyone was supposed to be free of inhibitions, none of that devil-may-care type of behavior seemed to happen around me.

In my senior year of high school, I worked for the local pharmacy. There was a girl that lived down the block who I'll call Alice. She was a year younger than me and moved in the summer before I started high school. I developed a huge crush on her (and a huge something else) once I noticed her round hips and generously proportioned bosom. She was not similarly enamored by my bow legs, excess body hair, braces, and nasally, whiny voice. My interest went unreturned. But, fast forward four years, and I'll be goddamned if she wasn't getting prescriptions for the pill at the pharmacy I worked in.

Her boyfriend was a guy a year ahead of me in

school. I'll call him Jim. One morning at the school bus stop, while I was a junior and Jim was a senior, I happened to overhear Jim tell someone about the college he was going to attend next fall. I had not heard of this particular institution of higher learning before and asked him why he had chosen it.

"Oh, I'm just going there to deal dope," he derisively replied. And this was the guy that Alice presumably was taking birth control for. How come she fell for a drug dealer and not a fine, upstanding young man like me who was on the school math team?

I'll share one more anecdote about this pharmacy job. The dad of a guy I went to school with was many of the local fathers who commuted by bus to Manhattan (as my own father did for many years). I'll call him Mr. Wilton. About once every two or three months, Mr. Wilton would come into the pharmacy and buy a 36-pack of Trojan brand condoms. 36! Back in those unenlightened times, condoms were kept behind the counter. When I waited on Mr. Wilton, he would have to tell me specifically what he wanted, and then I would fetch them for him.

Why, I thought to myself, since he worked in New York, *couldn't he buy his condoms there?* Mr. Wilton was a quiet, unassuming man, so I don't think he was trying to show off the frequency by which he was banging Mrs. Wilton, a mom in the neighborhood who had served me juice and cookies on more than one occasion. I dreaded the few times I had to wait on him during that year in the pharmacy. Maybe he *was* showing off.

Chapter 48: Humans Are Animals

I'm just about worthless if I get more than two consecutive bad nights of sleep. I also tend to try to drift off into dreamland after lunch and can't survive without an afternoon cup of coffee. I get lightheaded on an empty stomach. Irregular bowel habits can impact my mood. I suspect that I am not alone in these qualities, as an awful lot of coffee, energy drinks, snacks, and laxatives are advertised on television. The fact is that all of the wonderful moral and intellectual qualities that we think define us as human are dependent upon keeping our bodies in working order. One of the reasons why people party with such gusto in high school and college is because they can get away with it and still function the next day. By the time you get to even as young as your late 20s, the hedonistic lifestyle takes a huge toll on the flesh.

When I was a kid, I thought that the typical older-adult emphasis on regular habits was boring and pointless. Now that I am one of those older adults myself, I realize that indeed it makes me boring, but it is anything but pointless.

My day typically starts at 6 a.m., after about eight hours of sleep. Breakfast consists of high fiber cereal and a glass of prune juice, followed by a cup of coffee. I then go through my stretching exercises at 6:30 a.m. as the stock market opens on the West Coast and I get a jump start on the day's news. That's followed by a visit to the bathroom accompanied by the morning paper, an event that occurs with such precision you could set your watch to it. Then there's a shower, shaving, and on days when necessary, a careful trimming of nose and ear hair. And with that, I am prepared to face the day because I am an animal and must have my bodily needs attended to before I can attain the grace of an angel. And you are an animal, too.

Chapter 49: Read It Like *The Dead Poets Society*

If by chance, you haven't seen the movie *The Dead Poets Society*, here is a quick plot summary. The movie is set in the year 1959. Robin Williams, in the role of John Keating, is hired to teach English at a private all-boys high school. He is a renegade in an era of conformity, who instructs his students to rip out the introduction to their poetry textbook so they can encounter the material with a fresh and open mind. He also urges them to *carpe diem*, Latin for "seize the day." Naturally, this being the black-and-white 1950s, and with all other adults around him totally closed-minded in their attitudes, he ends up alienating himself to the rest of the faculty and the school administration.

A student in his class, Neil, (spoiler alert) loves the theater. However, he has a domineering father who makes him deeply unhappy. The dad, played by Kurtwood Smith, insists that Neil go to medical school and specifically forbids him to participate in the school play, since as a future doctor he needs to focus his full attention on academics. Neil, against his father's wishes, auditions for the role of Puck in a *Midsummer Night's Dream* and wins the part. Dad discovers his son's defiance, and in a rage, orders him to quit the production and never disobey him again. That night, the son, despondent because he cannot follow his dream, commits suicide. Predictably, his act is blamed on Mr. Keating for putting crazy ideas into the students' heads. The administration takes quick action, and the unconventional teacher is fired.

While the movie itself is quite entertaining, for me the real lesson is how the John Keating character tells his students to approach the classics of literature. He believes literature should be experienced firsthand before its meaning is "explained."

I finished high school at age 18 but did not start college until 21, and during those three years, I read voraciously. Free from the burden of school, I loved that I had no assigned reading, and I followed my heart. Most of the works I pored over were picked up at second-hand bookshops or borrowed from fellow backpackers, so the cost was trivial. If I started a new book and got bored 5 or 10 pages in, then I simply put it down and read something else, even it if was supposed to be a classic. (I still have yet to get beyond the first 50 pages of *Pride and Prejudice*.)

I recall reading *The Adventures of Huckleberry Finn*, still one of my favorite books. I served as a volunteer on a kibbutz at the time, and I had a roommate who was a recent college graduate. He shared with me his professor's perspective on the book's many flaws, which he had read in an American literature class. I remember thinking to myself, *Who cares? I am going to read it on my own terms and take whatever meaning from it I can.*

During those three years, I must have read over 100 books, many of them great works, such as most of the writings of George Orwell. I felt my mind being shaped and influenced directly by each author without a teacher or professor telling me what the book was "supposed" to mean. I am grateful for having had that opportunity.

Whenever possible, try to experience a creative work without too much information beforehand. Oh, and *carpe diem*.

Chapter 50: Land Ho!

Life is a journey, and we are often lost at sea along the way. Our parents and teachers gave us advice while we were growing up. In some cases, they were well-intentioned. At other times, like many of my high school teachers, they were indifferent, seemingly more concerned about a paycheck and getting one year more of vesting toward their pension than they were about the students in their charge. But even when the advice I received was good, it was still often only appropriate to a particular time. In the 1970s, the path to career success generally involved a job with a big company. Some key skills included dressing well, punctuality, and being able to use the correct fork and order off of a wine list with a modicum of sophistication. A cabernet sauvignon goes well with steak, a chardonnay pairs nicely with swordfish, and a chianti would be a good choice for pasta. That knowledge would probably be of little use in advancing your career at a software company, where the developers might live on tacos, Hot Pockets, and energy drinks.

The world changes, and what worked for one generation may not be quite as productive for the next. Once, there were rules for everything. And many of those rules are now obsolete.

And so I entered adult life unprepared. As I progressed through high school and college, much of the material we studied enabled further progress to the next rung up on the education ladder. And in many disciplines, such as the humanities, scaling the summit and earning a Ph.D. usually prepares one for a career in academia.

Recognizing how little value formal education often contains, I have tried to provide some advice in this book on how to compensate for the gap between what you need to know to deal with adult life and what you were taught in school. I hope I have been helpful. I believe that what most people want in life is some measure of happiness and loving relationships with other people. The vast quantity of information we are forced to absorb in school is of little value in helping us achieve these goals. Much of life post-school is spent learning the information needed to become a successful, well-functioning adult, not factoring equations with techniques we learned at age 14.

I knew nothing about relationships, the work world, or the challenges of adult life when I finished school. I wouldn't say I am an expert today, but at least I am less ignorant.

Like a baby that learns to walk, every misstep and stumble is an exercise in becoming more proficient. I have had more than my fair share of stumbles myself, but each time I try to get back on my feet and continue the learning process.

Ultimately, we all get our wisdom the hard-earned way, and I hope you are now a little bit closer to achieving yours.

The End

NOTES

Preface

1. "Demographics," US Environmental Protection Agency, April 14, 2013, http://www.epa.gov/agriculture/ag101/demographics.html.

Chapter 3

2. "Fertility rate, total, births per woman," The World Bank, September 14, 2013, http://data.worldbank.org/indicator/SP.DYN.TFRT.IN?page=6.
3. The World Factbook, Central Intelligence Agency, September 16, 2013, https://www.cia.gov/library/publications/the-world-factbook/rankorder/2127rank.html.
4. "GDP per capita growth, (annual %)," The World Bank, September 14, 2013, http://data.worldbank.org/indicator/NY.GDP.PCAP.KD.ZG.
5. Global and regional food consumption patterns and trends, World Health Organization, September 20, 2013, http://www.who.int/nutrition/topics/3_foodconsumption/en/.
6. Johnson, Keith and Gold, Russell, "US Oil Notches Record Growth," The Wall Street Journal, (New York, NY), June 12, 2013, http://online.wsj.com/news/articles/SB1000

1424127887324049504578541601909939628.

7.   "Our Nation's Air: Status and Trends Through 2010," US Environmental Protection Agency, Office of Air Quality Planning and Standards, 2011, 1-32.

Chapter 6

8.   "Median Age at First Marriage, 1890-2010," Infoplease, September 20, 2013, http://www.infoplease.com/ipa/A0005061.html.

Chapter 8

9.   "The Dental Access Gap: Findings from a National Survey," Lake Research Partners, September 21, 2013, http://www.google.com/url?sa=t&rct=j&q=&esrc=s&source=web&cd=1&ved=0CC4QFjAA&url=http%3A%2F%2Fwww.wkkf.org%2F~%2Fmedia%2F00e17806d74e45d6be6a6fe8eca1a89a%2Fwkkf%2520oral%2520health%2520survey_2011.pdf&ei=Oyo3UvO1PM_0igLq94AI&usg=AFQjCNFDlO8SSGlUcM2FX1KxqC1RlN3S6Q&sig2=YA-89Zvk74CxuYk-woc39w&bvm=bv.52164340,d.cGE.

Chapter 17

10. "Digest of Education Statistics: 2011, National Center of Education Statistics," US Department of Education, October 4, 2013, http://nces.ed.gov/programs/digest/d11/.

Chapter 25

11. Maraniss, David. Barack Obama: The Story (New York: Simon & Schuster, 2012), 293-294.

Chapter 26

12. Pinker, Steven. The Blank Slate: The Denial of Human Nature (New York: Penguin Books, 2012), 374-377.

Chapter 28

13. Beamon, Todd and Bachman, John, "Rep. Steve King Slams Norquist Over Attacks on Immigration," Newsmax, July 18, 2013, http://www.newsmax.com/Newsfront/king-norquist-attacks-immigration/2013/07/18/id/515882.

Chapter 30

14. Dawkins, Richard. The Selfish Gene (New York: Oxford University Press, 1976).

Chapter 32

15. Thomas, Lewis. The Lives of a Cell: Notes of a Biology Watcher (New York: The Viking Press, Inc., 1974).

16. Worldwide Smart Connected Device Market Crossed 1 Billion Shipments in 2012, Apple Pulls Near Samsung in Fourth Quarter, According to IDC, IDC, March 26, 2013. Accessed October 5, 2013, http://www.idc.com/getdoc.jsp?containerId=prUS24037713.

Chapter 36

17. Than, Ker, "Symmetrical Bodies are More Beautiful to Humans," *National Geographic*, August 18, 2008. Accessed September 25, 2013, http://news.nationalgeographic.com/news/2008/08/080818-body-symmetry.html.

Chapter 37

18. Solomon, Nancy,"40 Years On, Newark Re-Examines Painful Riot Past," NPR, July 14, 2007. Accessed October 3, 2013, http://www.npr.org/templates/story/story.php?storyId=11966375.

19. Amos, Jason, "GOOD NEWS FOR GRADUATION RATES: Nation's High School Graduation Rate Highest Since 1974," Alliance for Excellent Education, January

28, 2013. Accessed October 6, 2013,
http://all4ed.org/articles/good-news-for-
graduation-rates-nations-high-school-
graduation-rate-highest-since-1974/.

Chapter 38

20. "Union Membership Declines in 2012,"
     United States Department of Labor, Bureau
     of Labor Statistics, January 24, 2013.
     Accessed October 6, 2013,
     http://www.bls.gov/opub/ted/2013/ted_2
     0130124.htm.

Chapter 43

21. Well, Ken and Levy, Ari. "Gore is Romney-
     Rich With $200 Million after Bush Defeat."
     Bloomberg, May 5, 2012. Accessed October
     25, 2013,
     http://www.bloomberg.com/news/2013-
     05-06/gore-is-romney-rich-with-200-
     million-after-bush-defeat.html.

Chapter 44

22. Bye, Jeffrey K. "Psychology Classics: Wason
     Selection Task (Part I)." Psychology in
     Action, October 7, 2012. Accessed October
     25, 2013,
     http://www.psychologyinaction.org/2012/

10/07/classic-psychology-experiments-
wason-selection-task-part-i/.

23. Ibid.

www.ingramcontent.com/pod-product-compliance
Lightning Source LLC
LaVergne TN
LVHW051052080426
835508LV00019B/1840